Prescription Drugs

Other books in the At Issue series:

At ✳ Issue

Prescription Drugs

Christine Watkins, *Book Editor*

Bonnie Szumski, *Publisher*
Helen Cothran, *Managing Editor*

GREENHAVEN PRESS
An imprint of Thomson Gale, a part of The Thomson Corporation

THOMSON
——✳——™
GALE

Detroit • New York • San Francisco • San Diego • New Haven, Conn.
Waterville, Maine • London • Munich

For more information, contact
Greenhaven Press
27500 Drake Rd.
Farmington Hills, MI 48331-3535
Or you can visit our Internet site at http://www.gale.com

Greenhaven Press anthologies primarily consist of previously published material taken from a variety of sources, including periodicals, books, scholarly journals, newspapers, government documents, and position papers from private and public organizations. These original sources are often edited for length and to ensure their accessibility for a young adult audience. The anthology editors also change the original titles of these works in order to clearly present the main thesis of each viewpoint and to explicitly indicate the opinion presented in the viewpoint. These alterations are made in consideration of both the reading and comprehension levels of a young adult audience. Every effort is made to ensure that Greenhaven Press accurately reflects the original intent of the authors included in this anthology.

Cover credit: © Brand X Pictures

LIBRARY OF CONGRESS CATALOGING-IN-PUBLICATION DATA

Prescription drugs / Christine Watkins, book editor.
    p. cm. — (At issue)
Includes bibliographical references and index.
ISBN 0-7377-3470-1 (lib. : alk. paper) — ISBN 0-7377-3471-X (pbk. : alk. paper)
    1. Drugs—Popular works. 2. Consumer education. I. Watkins, Christine, 1951– . II. At issue (San Diego, Calif.)
RM301.15.P734 2006
615'.1—dc22   2005052723

Printed in the United States of America

Contents

Introduction

Most Americans believe that prescription drugs benefit society by saving lives, increasing productivity at work, and improving quality of life. According to a 2005 Kaiser Family Foundation report, 72 percent of Americans surveyed said that prescription drugs made a "big difference" in the lives of people with chronic conditions such as heart disease, and 91 percent responded that the development of new drugs is an important contribution to society. Indeed, pharmaceutical companies are discovering how to prevent normal cells from becoming malignant, developing drugs that will prevent debilitating conditions like rheumatoid arthritis and inflammatory bowel syndrome, and researching treatments for devastating diseases such as AIDS. Although prescription drugs offer many valuable benefits, they remain controversial because of their possible health risks, the problem of abuse, and the proliferation of illegal prescription drug sales over the Internet.

The rising number of reports about the potentially harmful side effects of prescription drugs has alarmed many Americans. For example, parents of children taking the antidepressant Paxil were horrified when they learned in 2003 that the drug might cause suicidal behavior. As well, when news stories broke in 2004 that the arthritis pain medications Vioxx and Celebrex can cause an increased heart attack risk, millions of Americans were stunned. Furthermore, some argue that the danger of side effects is widespread. As health consultant and researcher Joan E. Gadsby writes in her book *Addiction by Prescription,* "Prescription drug adverse reactions are the third leading cause of death in America, affecting an estimated 200,000 people each year."

As a result of reports about prescription drugs such as Paxil and Vioxx, some lawmakers and consumer advocates are accusing the U.S. Food and Drug Administration (FDA) of not monitoring these drugs adequately to protect the public health. In response, Steven Galson, acting director of the FDA Center for Drug Evaluation and Research (CDER), said his agency has "taken the criticism to heart" and has begun to make changes to improve its safety regulations and keep consumers informed about the possible risks of drugs. To that end, the FDA has begun issuing alerts on its Web site about emerging drug-safety concerns. It also plans to create an independent drug-safety board and to actively seek feedback from medical experts and patients on how best to publicize information about the risks of prescription drugs. In addition, drug companies have agreed to register all drug trials and post their results—negative as well as positive—on a public database, creating a new level of openness about drug research.

In addition to the issue of drug safety, many Americans are concerned about the escalation of abuse of prescription drugs. "The nonmedical use of prescription drugs has become an increasingly wide-spread and serious problem in this country," said John P. Walters, director of the White House Office of National Drug Control Policy (ONDCP). According to the 2002 National Survey on Drug Use and Health, 6.2 million Americans abused prescription drugs that year. Of those, more than 70 percent abused painkillers, including opioids, drugs that have the characteristics of opiate narcotics but which are not derived from opium. Because of their euphoric effect, opioids are right behind marijuana as the drug of choice among teenagers and young adults. Some experts are particularly concerned about opioids because long-term use can lead to addiction and fatal overdoses. The admission in 2003 by well-known radio host Rush Limbaugh of his addiction to the prescription painkiller OxyContin—a trade name for the opioid oxycodone hydrochloride—helped bring this problem of prescription drug abuse to the public's attention.

Prescription drug abuse has become an even more difficult problem to solve in recent years because thousands of illegal Internet pharmacies are springing up at an alarming rate, enabling customers to easily obtain the pharmaceuticals they want without a valid prescription or guidance from a doctor. In 2001, California teenager Ryan Haight died in his bedroom after inadvertently overdosing on a mixture of pills, including the powerful painkiller Vicodin, which he obtained from an illegal Internet pharmacy. In New Jersey in 2003, nineteen-year-old Jason Surks accidentally overdosed on the anti-anxiety medication Xanax that he had purchased from rogue Mexican Internet pharmacies. Jason's father Mark Surks said, "All he had to do was point his Internet browser at any number of Web sites . . . I think he looked at these drugs as safe."

Despite the risks and problems of abuse, prescription drugs

do help many Americans: 50 million chronic pain sufferers rely on prescription medication to relieve their pain and to maintain a somewhat normal life. To balance the need for effective pain treatment with the need to prevent abuse of prescription drugs, the government is considering safety programs to ensure that only the appropriate patients receive the medication; to educate physicians, pharmacies, and the public about the safe use of opioids; and to monitor for potential abuse problems. Former FDA commissioner Mark B. McClellan states that the "FDA's job is to maximize the potential benefits that patients receive from these drugs while, at the same time, minimizing the risks associated with these products."

To address the problem of prescription drug abuse, House Government Reform Committee chairman Tom Davis, a Republican representative from Virginia, introduced the Internet Pharmacy Consumer Protection Act of 2005. This legislation would require Internet pharmacies to identify the business, physicians, and pharmacists associated with their Web sites, and would prohibit Internet pharmacies from referring a customer to a doctor who writes prescriptions without ever seeing the patient. John Walters said the act "is an important step in protecting the integrity of our medical system and in keeping families safe."

However, even drug manufacturers warn that no drug is completely safe. And there are a number of people—including the one-time dean of Harvard Medical School, Oliver Wendell Holmes—who believe that pharmaceuticals do more harm than good. Holmes said, "I firmly believe that if the whole *material medica* [all available drugs] could be sunk to the bottom of the sea, it would be all the better for mankind, and all the worse for the fishes." At the same time, research has shown that most Americans value their prescription drugs and believe that their benefits outweigh their risks. The viewpoints in *At Issue: Prescription Drugs* offer a variety of perspectives on this controversial and passionately debated subject.

1

Prescription Drug Prices Are Excessive

Katharine Greider

Katharine Greider is a journalist and investigative reporter. She also is the author of the book The Big Fix: How the Pharmaceutical Industry Rips Off American Consumers.

The major pharmaceutical companies (Big Pharma) charge such high prices for their products that their profit margins exceed those of the biggest oil and entertainment companies. When the public cries out for lower drug prices, the industry representatives respond that the result would be inadequate funding for research of lifesaving drugs. This response by pharmaceutical industry spokespeople implies that their high profits are invested in the development of new cures for deadly diseases. However, in recent years drug companies have developed few breakthrough drugs. Instead, it appears that Big Pharma is focused on commercial gain, developing profitable drugs for minor problems such as baldness rather than cures for serious diseases like malaria, which kills thousands of people worldwide.

"America's Pharmaceutical Companies: New Medicines. New Hope." This was the tag line of full-page ads appearing in national magazines last year [2002] as part of a campaign by drug-industry trade group Pharmaceutical Research and Manufacturers of America (PhRMA) to gussy up its increasingly negative image. The ads featured handsome, smiling people in lab coats—just some of the "50,000 researchers at America's pharmaceutical companies [who are] dedicating their lives to making all our lives better." Perusing its promotional materials, you might get the idea the pharmaceutical industry is a non-profit research operation out to save the human race by putting every disease that afflicts us "on the path to extinction," as one industry spokesperson put it.

But this message of hope has a dark side. Faced with a proposal to limit drug prices, industry representatives invariably respond by insisting the measure will put an end to research into terrifying diseases like Alzheimer's and cancer, hitting us where we live. "I can guarantee," PhRMA's Richard Smith warned reporters last year [2002], ("If you aren't already today, at some point in your lives every one in this room will be a patient in need of medical care. The question is: Will a medicine be there for you?")

Here is the industry driving home its point: "'If you touch our profits, the laboratories will close and you'll all die,'" says Alan Sager, a professor of health services at Boston University School of Public Health who has studied the drug industry. "It's a terror tactic."

Drug Companies Blame Research and Development

Certainly pharmaceutical companies take on risk by spending very large sums in their laboratories. Comparing numbers from PhRMA's annual member survey with government appropriations, the Federation of American Societies for Experimental Biology estimates that big pharmaceutical companies sponsored 47 percent of all biomedical R&D [research and development] in 2000. This represented a huge increase in R&D spending by Big Pharma [large pharmaceutical companies] in the latter half of the 1990s, with the government's share of total R&D declining to 39 percent despite substantial increases in the National Institutes of Health (NIH) budget.

// If you touch our profits, the laboratories will close and you'll all die. //

But some frankly doubt PhRMA's figures, derived from confidential reports by member companies. Though pharma execs

hold up R&D spending as a justification for just about everything they do, they hold the details of this spending very close
to the chest. Examinations by various advocacy groups of drugmakers' financial reports have yielded much lower estimates of
their R&D budgets. For example, while manufacturers reported
spending over $20 billion on R&D in 1999, Sager and colleague
Deborah Socolar arrive at "a more skeptical estimate," based on
financial filings, of about $10 billion.

> *The big drug companies have managed to develop drugs and sell them at higher profit margins than are enjoyed by the biggest oil companies, entertainment companies, auto makers and commercial banks.*

Perhaps more important than the question of how much
companies spend on R&D—assume it's a large and increasing
amount—is what those drug-development dollars are yielding.
After all, in asserting the need to charge high prices for drugs,
industry spokespeople implicitly suggest their R&D has enormous social value—that it proffers "new hope" to the sick and
dying. And indeed few would deny that the history of the
pharmaceutical industry is, in part, the history of human
progress: from vaccines to antibiotics and, more recently, an array of AIDS drugs, some medicines have produced benefits beyond measure. But brush aside the industry platitudes about
new cures for a close look at products coming through R&D
pipelines, and one finds that too often their value is more commercial than social.

The Drug Industry Focuses on Commercial Gain

Well over half the drugs approved in the United States between
1989 and 2000 were "product-line extensions" using old active
ingredients, according to a study released in May 2002 by the
National Institute for Health Care Management. As the pace of
new drug approvals accelerated sharply over the past decade,
"standard-rated" product-line extensions—those deemed by
the US Food and Drug Administration (FDA) to add no significant benefit over already available drugs—accounted for 62

percent of this growth. These standard-rated product-line extensions also contributed most to increased consumer spending on new drugs in the five years leading up to 2000. With true breakthroughs few and far between, drug companies are flooding the market with new dosages, new combinations and otherwise rejiggered forms of their older medicines.

Generally speaking the drug industry does not expend resources to develop medicines that might be an enormous boon for public health but offer little prospect for commercial gain. For example, a tiny percentage of new drugs brought to market are to treat diseases like malaria that kill huge numbers of poor people around the world. If this seems natural enough—these are businesspeople after all, not public-health activists—then perhaps it will seem more surprising that American taxpayers support a portion of the research to develop drugs over which drug companies claim sole proprietorship. Proprietorship and, of course, the right to charge whatever they please. . . .

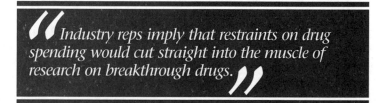

Industry reps imply that restraints on drug spending would cut straight into the muscle of research on breakthrough drugs.

At the end of the day, industry poor-mouthing about the burdens of drug R&D is unconvincing for a simple reason: For decades, pharmaceuticals has been one of the most profitable businesses in America. While the average Fortune 500 company saw declining profits in a difficult environment in 2001, drug companies on the list actually boosted their profits by 33 percent, according to an analysis of Fortune 500 data by Public Citizen [a consumer advocacy organization]. These titan drugmakers took 18.5 percent of revenues as profit—eight times the median for all other Fortune 500 companies. In other words, whatever the unique exigencies of pharmaceutical R&D, the big drug companies have managed to develop drugs and sell them at higher profit margins than are enjoyed by the biggest oil companies, entertainment companies, auto makers and commercial banks. . . .

In the meantime, the weight of Big Pharma is one that Americans have borne and continue to bear disproportionately. Our "free pricing," vast population and sky's-the-limit demand are what drive drug profits worldwide. Of course, even this basic fact creates occasion for dispute. While many consumer groups and politicians say it's our prices that are out of whack, industry supporters insist other wealthy consumers—the Europeans and the Japanese, for example—should pay more for drugs, and that their refusal to do so, unfair as it is, leaves the responsibility for R&D in American hands. There it is again: Do anything to curtail costs in the United States, and you can forget about a cure for Alzheimer's.

Perhaps there's another way to look at it. The drug industry's higher-than-average profits—the pot of gold at the end of the rainbow—has fueled increasing investments in R&D. This means that, as in other businesses, the consumer not only pays the cost of making the product but subsidizes the growth of the industry itself. That the drug industry has managed to elevate its development effort to the status of sacred cow—touch it and lives will be lost—obscures a slew of important questions. Have all these R&D dollars been efficiently deployed from a business standpoint, much less from the public's point of view? Does the industry really need to grow at a double-digit clip in order to produce medicines and make money? In the past ten years R&D spending grew at about 13 percent per year, says Princeton economist Uwe Reinhardt. This rate of increase, he calculates, gets you to $595 billion by the year 2025. "The question I raise is, Well, who's to say that's the right number? And then the pharmaceutical industry says, Well, the market." But when buyers try to limit drug spending—when state governments establish methods for bargaining down prices under Medicaid, for example—drugmakers tend not to accept these efforts as reflecting the wisdom of a free market. As Reinhardt observes, "When the market responds, they scream."

Drug Companies Should Focus on Public Health

If the outcome of the industry's profit-driven R&D is especially stark in poorer nations, nothing guarantees that it reflects the public-health priorities even of wealthy Americans. Do we really want to pay for the invention of baldness remedies instead of getting more important drugs at lower cost so they could help more people? If we were in charge, would we order Pfizer's rivals to get cracking on something to compete with Viagra (as a number have done) or with cholesterol-reducing Lipitor (already in a crowded class)? Obviously we don't get to make these calls; we don't even have access to information that would let us lay it all on the table and see where R&D resources are being spent. All we do is sign the checks. Have American consumers, disgruntled about costs but confident our dollars were going to Project Banish Disease, in fact been drafted into Operation Grow Big Pharma? Are we really to believe they're one and the same?

Industry reps imply that restraints on drug spending would cut straight into the muscle of research on breakthrough drugs. But others point to drug-company budget items where there seems to be plenty of fat: profits yes, but also, and more important, marketing. Consumer advocate Families USA found that in 2000 and 2001, the nine companies selling the most drugs to American seniors spent more money—in most cases more than twice as much—on marketing and administration than on R&D. Indeed, whether their increasing R&D investments pan out or disappoint, drugmakers will work assiduously—because they're businesses and not public-health advocates—to recoup those investments and sustain high earnings growth by selling lots of product to American consumers. And friends, they have ways of doing that.

2

Prescription Drug Prices Are Fair

Doug Bandow

Doug Bandow is a senior fellow at the Cato Institute, a libertarian think tank in Washington, D.C. He is also a nationally syndicated columnist with Copley News Service. He has written several books and has appeared on numerous television programs, including ABC Nightly News *and* CNN's Crossfire.

The American pharmaceutical industry has benefited the world beyond measure. Instead of expressing gratitude for the lifesaving and life-improving products that the industry provides, consumers and politicians denounce drugmakers for charging unreasonably high prices. However, the prices are not excessive considering the benefits the drugs offer. Without strong profits, the research and development of breakthrough medicines would not be possible. The proposed solutions to reduce pharmaceutical costs—such as mandatory price ceilings and restrictions on patents—could ruin a world-leading, vital industry.

Few sectors of the economy have provided more benefits to consumers than the pharmaceutical industry. Drugmakers have been vilified by patients and politicians alike, however, because of what they see as unreasonably high drug costs. Yet, medicine is not the most important component of the recent rise in health care expenses. Morever, the primary reason for current increases in total drug costs is that more and more people are using newer medicines—which means that con-

Doug Bandow, "Demonizing Drug Makers: The Political Assault on the Pharmaceutical Industry," *USA Today Magazine,* vol. 132, September 2003, p. 30. Copyright © 2003 by the Society for the Advancement of Education. Reproduced by permission.

sumer benefits are rising even faster

Simplistic comparisons between drug costs in the U.S. and those in other countries have little value. Economic wealth, exchange rates, product liability roles, price controls, and other factors all contribute to the price of drugs. More important, prices for U.S. pharmaceuticals are not excessive relative to the benefits they offer. Drugs have contributed to the sharp reduction in mortality rates from many diseases, including AIDS. Pharmaceuticals also reduce the cost of alternative treatments. Thus, restricting access to the newest and best drugs can be economically counterproductive.

High Profits Go to Research and Development

However, the only way to develop new drugs is to invest heavily in research and development. The $30,000,000,000 spent annually by U.S. drugmakers dwarfs the budget of the National Institutes of Health and investments by foreign drug companies. Profits of U.S. firms tend to be high, but not uniformly so, and they create a "virtuous cycle" that encourages more research and development to create groundbreaking medicine.

Yet, industry critics propose everything from socialized medicine to price controls and limits on patents. Such measures would reduce incentives to create new medicines. It is true that some people, especially poor individuals in less-developed countries, lack sufficient access to pharmaceuticals. Private charity at home and abroad should make them more available to those who are most in need, and Washington should include a drug benefit as part of overall Medicare reform. In the meantime, states should help needy seniors through limited pharmaceutical access programs. In addition, policymakers must avoid taking steps that would, intentionally or not, wreck a world-leading industry and deny people access to life-saving medicines.

Many Americans owe their health and lives to new products that emerge on a regular basis from the pharmaceutical industry. In the coming years, genetic research is likely to dramatically expand the benefits of pharmaceutical R&D [research and development]. One might fairly expect most people, especially those who are ill, to be grateful. However, demonstrators around the world are targeting the pharmaceutical industry, apparently for daring to sell the AIDS drugs that it created at high cost. The tome for the war on "Big Pharma" [large pharmaceutical companies] was set in the 2000 presidential race, when then–Vice Pres. Al Gore campaigned against drugmakers with faux populist rhetoric: "Big tobacco, big oil, the big polluters, the pharmaceutical companies, the HMOs, sometimes you have to be willing to stand up and say no, so families can have a better life." It was an astonishing comparison that equated companies that make life-saving products with those that often are accused of harming consumers. Yet, in the same speech, the Vice President acknowledged "a time of almost unimaginable medical breakthroughs"—produced by the very companies he was attacking. . . .

Politicians Attack Drug Companies

On what seems to be a daily basis, both Federal and state politicians are putting forward proposals for various terms of price controls, patent invalidations, and advertising restrictions. The hunt is on for more generous drug benefits at lower prices. A potentially unprecedented expansion of the Medicare entitlement in the form of prescription drug benefits has become the top domestic policy issue in Congress. Whether those benefits will be managed in private competitive markets or subjected to centralized price controls remains to be seen. State legislators faced with bloated Medicaid program budgets have latched onto high drug prices as the key culprit. The political appetite for increased Medicare and Medicaid drug benefits shows no sign of abating. Many officeholders hope to feed it with a steady diet of mandatory price ceilings, weakened patent rights, and restrictive drug formularies (lists of covered and preferred drugs). Increasingly, policymakers treat the innovative drug industry like a political piñata—whacking it with accusations and threats while expecting it to yield its treasured prizes.

Others fault drug companies for advertising their wares too directly and aggressively to consumers, claiming that such advertising merely increases purchases of high-priced "me-too" drugs that offer little therapeutic advantage over cheaper and older ones. Many drugmakers also are accused of exploiting legal loopholes to extend their patented drug monopolies well beyond reasonable bounds.

Even in the aftermath of the fall 2002 elections, which restored Republican Party control of both Houses of Congress and a marginally more favorable Capitol Hill climate for the pharmaceutical industry, the crusade against drug companies continues. The heat is still on brand-name drugmakers to yield more of their profits and the patent rights that protect them so that generic imitators can flood the market with lower-cost versions of today's drugs and officeholders can dispense them more widely to public health program beneficiaries.

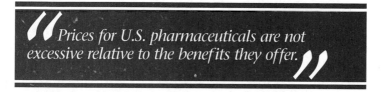

Prices for U.S. pharmaceuticals are not excessive relative to the benefits they offer.

Whether the issues ahead are indirect price controls, coerced "discounts," dilution of patent rights, reimportation of U.S.-manufactured drugs from lower-priced foreign markets, or just plain old-fashioned political scapegoating, the common focus is to force down prices. Under one guise or another, government would confiscate revenue from firms, in effect seizing their property. . . .

Alas, drug industry critics have gotten the issue almost entirely wrong, from the statistics they cite to the solutions they promote. Their insistence on crude government intervention to lower drug prices, rather than dynamic market-based innovations to improve our overall health, risks killing the goose that lays the golden eggs.

Despite conventional political assumptions, prescription drugs are not the driving force behind rising health care costs. In fact hospital care costs were the most important component of rising health care expenses in 2001, accounting for 51% of the increase. Nor are costs rising so fast because drugmakers are hiking prices. It only seems so because, as the old adage goes, if you torture statistics long enough, they will confess to anything.

The Benefits Exceed the Costs

A narrow emphasis on the cost of prescription drugs is misguided. Prices cannot be debated in isolation. Drugs do not simply represent unnecessary expenses that need to be controlled (although medical professionals are as apt as patients to think in these terms). Even though the steadily increasing demand for drugs drives up their prices and overall cost, that demand reflects the premium that Americans place on improved well-being.

Consumers demand pharmaceuticals because they offer enormous benefits. Some 400 new drugs ended up on the market during the 1990s because people desired them, just as they wanted thousands of other new products—computers, software, cell phones, autos, SUVs, and much, much more. The highest-priced drugs do not represent luxury goods; they address serious and painful conditions. About half of the $22,500,000,000 increase in retail drug spending in 2001 occurred among just nine categories of medicines—those used to treat depression, high cholesterol, diabetes, arthritis, high blood pressure, pain, allergies, ulcers, and other gastrointestinal ailments.

There are 122 drugs under development for heart diseases and strokes. Another 256 medicines will target infectious diseases of all sorts, including hepatitis, pneumonia, staph infections, and sexually transmitted diseases like herpes and gonorrhea. A number of vaccines, ranging from improved polio compounds to new treatments to prevent cocaine addiction, Alzheimer's, and traveler's diarrhea, are in process as well. Drugs also are being developed to combat conditions such as high cholesterol, psoriasis, and obesity. Even something as simple as an antihistamine to ameliorate an allergy for cat hair can dramatically improve the quality of life. One can look at the benefits another way: 358 medicines under development address more than 30 diseases that disproportionately afflict women.

By one estimate, new prescription drugs accounted for 45% of the variation of the reduction in mortality among different diseases between 1970 and 1991. Longevity has increased seven years since 1960 alone. According to Columbia University Graduate School of Business professor Frank Lichtenberg, "On average, each new drug approved, during the period 1970–91 is estimated to have saved 11,200 life-years . . ." and presumably continued to do so in subsequent years. Medicines do more than extend lives, though. They improve the quality of lives—not just the patients', but those of their family members and other caregivers. Pharmaceutical products provide economic benefits, too. They reduce medical expenditures by, for example, lowering the rate of hospitalizations, surgeries, and other invasive medical treatments.

Price Restrictions Will Hurt Patients

Since new, better, and more expensive medicines are considered to be a problem, American politicians have come up with a host of counterproductive "solutions." The most common is price controls, though other favorites include stripping away patent protection, limiting advertising, and expanding taxpayer-financed subsidies.

Price controls can be direct or indirect. Certain proposals would link U.S. prices to foreign levels; others would limit the costs of drugs purchased as part of Federal or state programs. Some creative state legislators would bring the nonpoor under Medicaid, which imposes price controls on pharmaceuticals.

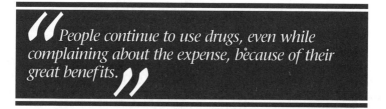

People continue to use drugs, even while complaining about the expense, because of their great benefits.

Most countries other than the U.S. are quite strict in that they regulate the prices of drugs, whether directly through price controls, or indirectly through limits on reimbursements under social insurance programs or through profit controls imposed on drug companies. Any form of price restriction tends to be inherently arbitrary and generates a host of unintended consequences. Whatever the official criteria are of a price control regime, warns John Calfee of the American Enterprise Institute, "decisions would be dominated by political forces, including managed care organizations, domestic versus foreign manufacturers, patient groups, insurance firms, employee benefit managers, labor unions, and other advocacy groups."

The general case against price controls is clear. Their experience running back to ancient times is extremely poor. They inflate demand, depress supply, create shortages, shift activity to unregulated sectors, and encourage wasteful avoidance and evasion activity. They also inevitably drift toward more complicated controls, entrench vested interests, take on a life of their own, and become extremely difficult to dismantle. Massive waiting lists, care delayed and denied, disincentives for research and development, and limited access to new technologies and treatments are standard. . . .

An Attack on Patents

Another fundamental assault on the pharmaceutical industry comes from those who would strip patent protection from drugs that generate the most social benefits. Some would erode patent rights to accelerate the market entry of lower-priced generic drug alternatives; others would do so to reduce the price of medicines that could counteract bioterrorism; and still others would do so to combat AIDS and other serious diseases in less-developed countries.

Patents give their owners the right to exclude others from making, using, or selling an invention for a fixed period of time. Drug manufacturers are in a unique position in that they cannot sell their patented products until they have successfully completed clinical trials and received Food and Drug Administration approval. The rising costs of prescription drug bills in recent years have triggered various complaints about brand-name companies exploiting legal loopholes to extend the patent life of their higher-priced drugs and delay competition from makers of cheaper generic drugs.

The Federal government's efforts to find a political balance between encouraging competition and allowing competition become more complex when its patent enforcement role collides with its financial stake as a major purchaser of prescription drugs. The temptation is to renege on its previously promised patent protection in order to arbitrarily drive down the prices it pays. Nevertheless, the only legitimate course of action is to consistently protect the regime of limited monopoly rights (patents) that it created. Federal officials should not get caught up in the fine-tuning, legal wrangling, and game playing over the terms and conditions of patents for innovative drugs. Policymakers should instead more consistently guarantee a set of fixed but limited torts for drug patents and thereby encourage the continued availability of investment capital needed for productive drug development. . . .

Advertising Benefits Consumers

Some industry critics want to control drug costs by restricting industry spending, especially on marketing. A particular target is direct-to-consumer (DTC) advertising. Some health care benefits managers complain that DTC ads cause excessive use of prescription drugs or that they steer consumers toward more expensive brand-name drugs. . . .

Disseminating information about new pharmaceuticals is an important mechanism for letting patients and doctors know what is available. One estimate is that more than 1,700 articles are published every year in each of 325 professional journals on the 25 leading medications. Marketing helps professionals keep afloat in this information flood. Moreover, what company in America makes a product and tells no one about it? Imagine General Motors developing a new car and keeping it secret.

The amount of mass media advertising directly aimed at patients remains relatively low—$2,800,000,000 in 2001, not much more than two percent of pharmaceutical sales. Yet, it has increased dramatically over the last decade, up from just $55,000,000 in 1991. Such advertising undoubtedly helps increase demand. That, in turn, has raised drug expenditures—treated by some bill payers as a negative in and of itself. However, people use medicines because the benefits exceed the costs. Increased demand makes products available that would otherwise be unprofitable. Thus, advertising does not compete with R&D; rather, the two are complementary. Marketing hikes revenues and investment returns, making more money available for and increasing incentive for research and development. Even as drugmakers advertise, they devote a larger share of sales to R&D than does the medical industry generally.

New Federal and state controls . . . would be hazardous to Americans' health.

Another criticism of DTC marketing is that ads are irrelevant or misleading, causing patients to demand products that are not good for them. As in any industry, ads vary in quality. Doctors remain a gatekeeper, though, often prescribing other brands, generics, older products, or nothing. Apparently some physicians begrudge their patients an explanation. Dr. Sandra Adamson Fryhofer of Emory University denounced drug ads because, "Not only do we have to take time to explain to these patients the nature of the medical problem they have, and whether it needs to be treated with drugs, but we also have to discuss whether the drug they have seen promoted is their best option." It's a curious objection. Physicians might occasionally find the duty to say no to be unpleasant, but their role, after all, is to serve patients, and they should be prepared to explain why a particular advertised drug is not appropriate.

In fact, advertising can play an important role in informing and empowering patients. That may be one reason why the

American Medical Association has suggested that the government ban ads. Expanded knowledge is particularly important in what traditionally has been a physician-led process: Patients can ask better questions and make better judgments if they know some of the options available.

Pharmaceuticals Provide Valuable Contributions

The fact that the typical "solutions" to reduce pharmaceutical prices would make Americans worse off does not mean that nothing should be done in response to concern over access and cost. Some people of limited means have trouble getting the drugs that they need. A wealthy and compassionate society should respond.

The principle that should govern any action, private or public, is "first do no harm." Government should not interfere with a pharmaceutical maker that works as well as it does only because it remains relatively free. Instead, remedies should be narrowly targeted to meet genuine needs. . . .

People continue to use drugs, even while complaining about the expense, because of their great benefits. Those benefits come only because profit-minded private firms are able to raise capital for R&D investments in the risky and uncertain business of pharmaceutical production. Marcia Angell and Arnold Relman of the Harvard Medical School argue that drugs are necessary for people's health and even their survival, yet "the drug companies often behave as though their only responsibility is to their shareholders." Of course, such an argument could be made for any health care provider, as well as farmers and even producers of other necessities, such as clothes and houses.

Yet, without pharmaceutical industry shareholders, there would be no companies and no R&D. Pharmaceutical firms are particularly important because they are entrepreneurial. Although profits are the driving economic force, that doesn't mean that the people who staff pharmaceutical companies don't desire to do good.

High costs pose a serious, but manageable, problem. Intrusive regulation and price controls would pose a far more serious, and far less manageable, situation. New drugs are saving countless lives today. New Federal and state controls, in contrast, would be hazardous to Americans' health. Government policy-makers must avoid taking steps that would, intentionally or not, wreck a world-leading industry and deny people access to life-saving medicines.

3

Direct Drug Advertising Undermines Health Care

Jerry Avorn

Jerry Avorn, an internist and drug researcher, is an associate professor of medicine at Harvard Medical School. He is one of the most frequently cited researchers in the fields of social science and medicine and has written many papers on medication use and its outcomes.

The United States is one of the few countries in which direct-to-consumer advertising of prescription drugs is permitted. Although this advertising may benefit Americans to some extent by increasing awareness of conditions such as depression, osteoporosis, and diabetes, the exorbitant cost of drug ads drives up the price of prescription drugs for patients. In addition, direct-to-consumer advertising can harm the doctor-patient relationship. Consumers who see commercials for brand-name drugs are likely to request prescriptions for these products from their doctors. It is often difficult for physicians to convince their patients that a more inexpensive generic drug will work just as well or that the requested drug is not appropriate for their condition. From a public health perspective, the millions of dollars drug companies spend every year on advertising would be better spent on communicating messages about diet, exercise, and substance abuse.

Patients may not have routine access to scientifically vetted information about their drugs when they fill their prescriptions, but they get plenty of input from advertising. Before the mid-1990s, many drug manufacturers were wary of entering the expensive world of consumer advertising, since promoting their products to doctors had traditionally been all that was needed to increase sales. But when HMOs [health maintenance organizations] sought to contain costs by restricting use of expensive drugs, the ground rules changed. The drug companies hoped that direct-to-consumer promotion could give them an unprecedented way to market their products to patients, bypassing both the physician and the managed care formulary committees. In 1997, the FDA [Food and Drug Administration] agreed to remove most prohibitions on such advertising.

Going Straight to the Consumer

A former FDA commissioner once asked whether such promotion was "misleading in a way that constitutes a public health hazard." In the disarmingly binary thinking that sometimes characterizes regulators, the agency declared that it was not. But a more interesting and important question is what effect this advertising has on the way medications are used in the United States. In nearly all other countries, such promotion is still not permitted; are we better off because we allow it?

In nearly all other countries, such promotion is still not permitted.

It's appealing to think that consumer ads might help patients detect diagnoses that have been unnoticed or undertreated by their physicians. After all, our health care system performs badly in the management of elevated cholesterol, hypertension, and diabetes, among many conditions. Other diagnoses suffer the dual liability of underdetection and undertreatment, including depression, incontinence, and osteoporosis. Advocates of pharmaceutical promotion raise an interesting point when they suggest that advertising to patients could increase awareness of these conditions and thus improve decisions on both sides of the prescription pad, a process that could in theory bring about an eventual public health benefit.

It is likely that some patients didn't know they were clinically depressed until they saw an ad for Zoloft, or weren't aware that there was a useful treatment for impotence until Bob Dole [1996 presidential candidate] told them so in a Viagra commercial. And it's also probably true that numerous patients found the courage to tell their doctors that they constantly wet themselves, and wanted treatment for it, only after they were exposed to promotion of a drug for incontinence. But from a public health point of view, is this the best way to spend $3 billion on health communications to the public? Even if more patients with high cholesterol or depression came into treatment because of ads for the costly drugs Lipitor or Prozac, how many more could have been treated using equally effective but much cheaper generic products in the same classes? And if the older thiazide drugs are both better and cheaper than many newer ones for the management of hypertension, what was the net public health benefit of all those costly ads for calcium-channel blockers, and the promotion-driven use of the expensive products that they generated?

Money for Advertising Could Be Better Spent

To fully assess the health impact of direct-to-consumer health communications, we would need to ask what the incremental benefit would have been had we spent some of those billions instead on messages about diet, exercise, or alcohol, drug, and tobacco abuse—or the importance of compliance with a prescribed drug regimen, regardless of which company manufactures the product. Perhaps some drug ads can make patients more informed consumers in some situations, and patient education and empowerment are in general good things. Yet some of the most lavish spending has been for overpriced products for heartburn and hay fever that were virtually identical to the expiring-patent products that preceded them. The real benefits of these drugs were high margins for their manufacturers, not improved outcomes for patients.

Direct-to-consumer ads can also have adverse effects on the doctor-patient relationship by turning the prescription into a kind of zero-sum negotiation between conflicting parties. The patient brandishes the latest glossy ad from *Newsweek* and demands the promoted product, while the doctor defends the original prescription—or just caves in altogether. The evidence indicates that for doctors faced with impossibly short visit times and reluctant to displease patients, the latter occurs more often. We needn't pine for the old days when the prescription was a sacrosanct gift bestowed by an omnipotent physician upon a grateful and unquestioning patient. But we are not benefited either if the transaction becomes an adversarial encounter, with doctor and patient circling each other warily in the consultation room, each trying to prevail over the other.

If we really want to increase the public's awareness of depression or incontinence or heart disease prevention, we could do so directly; those same talented people at the advertising agencies would be quite willing to put together promotions that are not product-specific if someone paid them to do so. If statins and antihypertensive drugs are underutilized (as they are), systems approaches to physician and patient noncompliance could work at least as well as, or better than, ads for specific products. Some might object that this is implausible—that pharmaceutical companies are willing to spend money to advertise their own products, but the nation itself lacks the resources to pay for public-interest medical messages. This is not true. In the end, the advertising bill is already being paid by the public. Patients, employers, insurance companies, and numerous government health care plans are ultimately providing the $3 billion spent on promotion to consumers, and more. It is not just the cost of all that airtime, the magazine pages, and the advertising firms that put the whole enticing package together. That is covered through the higher drug prices needed to pay for such expensive advertising. It is also the cost of using a more expensive patented product when nearly identical generics are available, and the cost of wasted physician time spent convincing a patient that her heartburn will respond as well to a generic drug as it would to the latest "purple pill." And it is the emotional cost to the cancer patient who learns that his fatigue and weakness are due to the malignancy itself, and will not disappear with a $1,500 dose of Procrit as the television commercials imply.

The Name of the Game Is Profits

The United States has made its choice about drug ads for patients, and it is unlikely that the genie can ever be put back in the bottle; defensible free-speech arguments and less defensible lobbying activities will guarantee that. We will probably see an increase in such advertising in the United States for the foreseeable future, even though most other nations seem able to run quite effective medical care systems without it. But somehow, the dollars aren't there for pro bono messages to educate the citizenry about medications. We lack the will to mount non-commercial programs on the same topics, and the health care system perceives that it cannot afford to do so. After all, it has trouble meeting its own rising costs for the current fiscal year—increases that ironically are caused in large part by rapidly swelling expenditures on these same heavily advertised drugs.

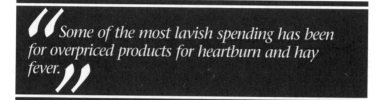

Some of the most lavish spending has been for overpriced products for heartburn and hay fever.

At issue is not the fact of pharmaceutical promotion, but the way it has come to have such a heavy influence on the drug choices made by doctors and patients. More ominous is a larger issue: these ads and commercials are helping to transform the medical care system from a professional enterprise focused on the health of people to just another marketplace, like those for fast food, cars, and pop music. The name of the game is buying as big a media splash as possible, catching the eye of the consumer, winning market share. The proliferation of this noise is simply another aspect of the commodification of medicine. It is born of our confused conviction that corporate self-promotion on all fronts is the most effective way to advance the health of the public. In this model, there is little room for health-oriented communications that don't advance a particular sales agenda.

Ironically, despite all the drug information lavished on patients by those who seek marketplace solutions to medical decisions, one kind of communication is strangely lacking—information for the consumer about what these products cost. Considering how central price information is in all other aspects of commerce, it's odd that its near-total absence from most brand-name drug ads has not been a topic of concern for most medical free-marketeers. They seem willing to endow drug decisions with only selected pieces of the free-enterprise model—heavy on information about benefits, light on risks, and nothing at all on cost.

But Americans are resourceful, and many have begun to use the internet to put the market to work in their own interest by searching out the best prices for a given drug. As we have seen, that search often leads outside our borders. But when patients seek to act on *that* kind of consumer information, the drug industry and federal government warn in strident terms against doing so. When consumers persisted in trying to be price-sensitive and buy American-made drugs from Canadian pharmacies, the first reaction of FDA and drug makers were threats to block the transactions and to shut down that open commerce.

We've seen that after FDA releases a drug for use, the molecule enters a world of laissez-faire chaos where normal scientific and economic standards suddenly loom small. Once the final wording on the package-insert label is negotiated, it is usually no one's job to make sure that prescribers know how the drug stacks up against the alternatives, or that we and our patients use it properly. But nature abhors vacuums of the informational as well as the physical kind. In the absence of a coherent societal agenda, others are more than happy to fill this cognitive space—with a free lunch thrown in as well. That vast sucking sound you hear is the pressure of commercial hype rushing in to fill the conceptual void.

4

Direct Drug Advertising Strengthens Health Care

Pharmaceutical Research and Manufacturers of America

Pharmaceutical Research and Manufacturers of America (PhRMA) represents the country's leading pharmaceutical research and biotechnology companies. PhRMA's mission is to advocate for public policies that encourage the discovery of new medicines.

Direct-to-consumer advertising (DTCA) is the term used for information that is provided by pharmaceutical companies to consumers. Surveys have shown that this direct marketing helps educate people about medical conditions and treatment options, improves the doctor-patient relationship by encouraging dialogue, and empowers patients to take an active role in their treatment. Although some consumers are concerned that the cost of DTCA drives up the price of prescription drugs, research shows that there is no correlation. Studies also show that pharmaceutical manufacturers spend much more money on research and development than on the marketing and promotion of their products.

While debate over prescription drug advertising, otherwise known as direct-to-consumer advertising (DTCA) is taking place now [2003], DTCA of prescription drugs is not new. The first print advertising designed to reach consumers started in the early 1960's. From the 1960's until the mid-1990's, most pharmaceutical advertising was confined to print—newspapers and magazines. In 1997, the Food and Drug Administration (FDA) issued a draft guidance that made possible electronic or broadcast advertising of prescription medicines. This draft guidance was finalized in 1999.

DTCA is a catchall phrase that refers to information provided by pharmaceutical manufacturers to consumers. Pharmaceutical manufacturers also provide, either directly or indirectly through physicians or pharmacists, brochures, newsletters, Internet sites and other materials about their products. The purpose of all of these materials is to educate consumers about diseases, about the symptoms that may help them identify the diseases, and the available therapies developed to treat them.

Research indicates that DTCA helps educate patients about medical conditions and treatment options, encourages dialogue between patients and physicians, prompts large numbers of Americans to discuss illnesses with their physicians for the first time and many others to do so earlier than they otherwise would have, and promotes improved compliance with physician-prescribed treatments.

Studies have also found that consumers like DTCA and benefit from it. It provides consumers with the information needed to ask their doctors questions about symptoms or new medicines that might help them. DTCA also reminds people to take medicines and get their prescriptions refilled when needed.

Despite what some critics suggest, there is no evidence that DTCA encourages inappropriate prescribing of prescription drugs. Utilization of pharmaceuticals is increasing for a multitude of reasons, including the aging population and the development of new and improved medicines, just to name a few. DTCA has an impact on drug usage, by encouraging patients to visit their doctor, often resulting in diagnosis of previously untreated illnesses, thereby allowing diseases to be treated early and avoid more costly treatment, surgery, and/or hospitalization. It may also increase patient compliance with physician-ordered treatment regimens.

There is no evidence to suggest that DTCA affects the price of medicine. To the contrary, studies that have examined this have found that there is no direct relationship between the amount of money spent on DTCA and price increases for a prescription drug.

DTCA strengthens the patient-physician relationship.

Physicians should and do remain in control of prescribing medicines. As a recent article in the *New England Journal of Medicine* makes clear, pharmaceutical companies recognize this by directing the large majority of their promotional activities toward physicians. Moreover, survey data consistently show that when patients ask a physician to prescribe a DTC-advertised medicine, many receive a different medicine or a non-pharmaceutical alternative. Preliminary results from the 2002 FDA survey of consumers found that, among the minority of respondents who said advertisements had caused them to talk with a physician and ask for a drug, less than half said their doctor gave them the prescription drug they asked about.

In a 2002 survey by *Prevention Magazine*, 50 percent of consumers who spoke with their doctor about an advertised medication received the drug. However, approximately 22 percent of consumers received a prescription for a medicine other than the one they asked about, while an additional 34 percent received no prescription at all.

DTCA's purpose is to encourage patients to talk to their physicians about their medical conditions and treatment options. In fact, every television advertisement for a prescription must include a message that viewers should ask their physician or pharmacist about the product. Such discussions are beneficial—for the patient in gaining an understanding of the physician's treatment recommendation, and for the physician in gaining a better understanding of the patient's needs. Notably, preliminary results from the 2002 FDA consumer survey found that most patients prompted by DTCA to discuss a drug with their doctor stated that their doctor welcomed the question (93%), discussed the drug with the patient (86%), and reacted as if the question were an ordinary part of the visit (83%).

The physician-patient relationship is strengthened, not weakened, when, as surveys show, DTCA prompts a patient to talk with a physician for the first time about a previously undiscussed condition (a 2000 Scott-Levin survey reports that 56% of physicians agree that "DTC advertising brings in patients to seek treatment that would otherwise go untreated"), improves patient compliance with physician-prescribed treatment regimens, or adds to patient information of medicines' risks and side effects and who should not take a drug. The 2002 *Prevention Magazine* survey found that 24.8 million Americans spoke with their doctor about a medical condition for the first time as a result of seeing a DTC advertisement.

A recent survey found that the majority of physician respondents believe that patients' awareness of DTC advertisements had a beneficial effect on office visits. Additional benefits of DTC advertising noted in the survey included:

- 85 percent of physicians treating high cholesterol conditions and 83 percent of physicians treating mood/anxiety disorders report that the drug discussed was appropriate for the patient.
- 54 percent of physicians treating high cholesterol conditions and 55 percent of physicians treating mood/anxiety disorders agree that the advertisement was influential in getting the patient to discuss their condition with a medical professional.
- For both high cholesterol and mood/anxiety disorders, 80 percent or more of physicians were satisfied with the outcome of office visits where advertisements were mentioned.

Another recent survey by Advanced Analytics and Guideline Consulting found that 55 percent of physicians surveyed rated overall DTC advertising as beneficial to patients, while 60 percent said that DTCA has had a positive impact on their own practice of medicine. Additionally:

- 80 percent of physicians indicated that advertisements describing a condition but no mention of a specific medication were beneficial to patients.
- 63 percent of physicians indicated that advertisements citing both a condition and a medication were beneficial to patients.

A survey by the National Medical Association (NMA), the nation's oldest and largest African-American medical association, representing more than 25,000 African-American physicians found that DTC advertisements raise disease awareness and bolster doctor-patient ties. According to NMA President, Dr. Lucille Perez:

> Doctors are finding that these ads are helping our patients talk to us about medical conditions they're at risk for. When you consider that the majority of drugs advertised can treat the diseases that disproportionately affect the African-American community, there is incredible potential. These ads can increase disease awareness that may be a beneficial tool to decrease the rampant disparities in the

health of the community. The NMA will advocate for increasing the awareness of the disease states in such advertisements. Further, we must view them as one of several tools that are potentially beneficial to the physician-patient dyad.

Advertising Empowers Consumers

In addition to encouraging discussion between patients and physicians, recent surveys indicate that DTCA makes consumers aware of new drugs and their benefits, as well as risks and side effects with the drugs advertised. The preliminary results from the FDA's 2002 consumer survey indicate:

- 90 percent of consumers surveyed recalled seeing television advertisements that contained information about the "benefits of the drug"
- 90 percent recalled information about "risks or side effects," and
- 89 percent recalled information about "who should not take the drug."
- 86 percent recalled "how to get more information."

A recent survey by Kaiser Family Foundation confirmed the FDA survey results. The Kaiser survey found that a large majority of those who viewed a DTC advertisement said that the advertisement did an excellent or good job telling them about the condition the medicine is designed to treat (84%), the potential benefits of the medicine (72%), and who should take the drug (66%).

As the earlier referenced *New England Journal of Medicine* article points out, DTCA is concentrated among a few therapeutic categories. These are therapeutic categories in which consumers can recognize their own symptoms, such as arthritis, seasonal allergies, and obesity; or for pharmaceuticals that treat chronic diseases with many undiagnosed sufferers, such as high cholesterol, osteoporosis, and depression; and for pharmaceuticals that enhance quality of life, such as those for skin conditions and hair loss. These advertisements help consumers recognize symptoms and seek appropriate care.

DTCA empowers consumers and enhances public health. The FDA has stated, "It [DTC advertising] is consistent with the whole trend toward consumer empowerment. We believe there is a certain public health benefit associated with letting people know what's available." A 1999 survey by *Prevention Magazine* found that consumers give high marks to pharmaceutical advertising. Of those surveyed, 76 percent felt DTC advertisements allowed them to become more involved in their own health care. The survey established that, "the benefits of DTC [direct-to-consumer] advertising could go far beyond simply selling prescription medicines: these advertisements play a very real role in enhancing the public health."

A recent study released by the National Health Council, whose constituency includes nearly 50 of the country's leading patient organizations representing nearly 100 million Americans with chronic diseases and/or disabilities, notes the positive impact DTCA can have, "The more information patients have, the more effective they can be in working with their doctor to make decisions about their health care. . . . The Council recognizes that DTC advertising provides important information to consumers and patients, which is beneficial to their health."

The benefits of advertising have been recognized by other elements of the health care sector who also advertise, including hospitals, doctors and insurers. Pharmaceutical manufacturers are not the only health care sector who advertises.

DTCA also appears to address a major problem in this country of undertreatment and underdiagnosis of disease. DTCA brings patients into doctors' offices and allows physicians to treat people who might otherwise go undiagnosed or untreated. For example, the 2002 *Prevention Magazine* survey found that 61.1 million Americans since 1997 were prompted by a DTC advertisement to talk to a doctor about a medical condition they previously had not discussed. According to DTC Monitor findings, 28 percent of those who contacted a doctor because of DTCA report that it was the *first time* they talked to their doctor about a condition. In addition, 22 percent reported that the advertising prompted them to talk to a doctor *earlier* than they would have otherwise.

Surveys of DTC advertisements for genital herpes provide compelling results. The Centers for Disease Control (CDC) estimate that 45 million Americans over age 12 carry the virus that causes genital herpes. Yet, only about 4.5 million Americans, or just one in ten, are being treated. Surveys indicate that DTC advertisements have helped increase the number of patients aware of the disease and have increased the number of newly diagnosed patients. For example, 34 percent of physicians surveyed by Scott-Levin stated that they had seen a significant increase in the number of newly diagnosed patients after advertisements for genital herpes began to air. In another survey, 67 percent of consumers who were aware of a genital herpes advertisement felt that the advertisements provided a valuable service in educating the public.

Patients Are Encouraged
to Discuss Their Symptoms

DTCA also encourages patients to discuss medical problems that otherwise may not have been discussed because it was either thought to be too personal or that there was a stigma attached to the disease. For example, a recent *Health Affairs* article examined the value of innovation and noted that new depression medications, known as selective serotonin reuptake inhibitors (SSRIs), that have been DTC advertised, have led to significant treatment expansion. Prior to the 1990's, it was estimated that about half of those persons who met a clinical definition of depression were not appropriately diagnosed, and many of those diagnosed did not receive clinically appropriate treatment. However, in the 1990's with the advent of SSRIs, treatment has been expanded. According to the article, "Manufacturers of SSRIs encouraged doctors to watch for depression and the reduced stigma afforded by the new medications induced patients to seek help." As a result, diagnosis and treatment for depression doubled over the 1990's.

Another benefit of DTCA is its ability to encourage compliance with physician-prescribed treatment regimens. Lack of compliance is a critical problem in achieving efficacious medical care. According to the 2002 *Prevention Magazine* survey, 17 percent of consumers said DTCA made it more likely (versus 2 percent less likely) they would take their medicine regularly and 12 percent of respondents reported that DTC advertisements made them more likely to refill prescriptions.

This is particularly important given the estimated costs of non-compliance. According to an article in the *Journal of Research Pharmaceutical Economics*, 5.5 percent of all hospital admissions are due to non-compliance, which results in $8.5 billion annually in unnecessary hospital expenditures, plus another $17–$25 billion in estimated indirect costs.

A June 2001 study by Pfizer and RxRemedy found that the percentage of diabetes, depression, elevated cholesterol, arthritis and allergy patients who remained on therapy after six months was significantly higher when the patient asked for a medicine with prompting from DTCA than when the patient was prescribed a medicine without such prompting. This suggests the advantages of consumers being involved with their health care and DTCA's role in encouraging such involvement.

Advertising Provides Accurate Information

Patients are increasingly turning to the growing volume of accessible health care information and thus, are moving us towards a more patient-focused health care system. Given this trend, DTCA is widely employed throughout our health care system—managed care organizations, hospitals and doctors all advertise to consumers. Unlike much other health care information, DTCA is subject to intense scrutiny for accuracy and balance by FDA regulators. Every DTCA—in print or electronic form—must:

- Be accurate and comply with the drug's FDA-approved labeling; and
- Contain "fair balance"—that is, an explanation of the risks and effectiveness of the drug.

Every print advertisement must include a detailed description of the risks. Every electronic advertisement must include a statement on the major risks and provide additional ways for consumers to obtain more information; this is called "adequate provision." Strict FDA requirements help make DTCA of prescription drugs reliable and accurate. . . .

Advertising Does Not Affect Drug Prices

Payers have questioned the effect of DTCA on prescription drug prices. However, the evidence shows there is no direct relationship between DTCA and the price growth of drugs. For example, one popular osteoarthritis drug had the highest DTC advertising spending of any brand-name medicine in 2000. However, the price increase from 1999 to 2000 was 3.9%, less than half a percent above the consumer price index (CPI). A common mood and anxiety disorder drug had no DTC advertising spending in 2000, but the price increase was roughly equal (3.1%) to the price increase for the most heavily advertised osteoarthritis drug. Neither price increase was out of line with CPI.

It's important to remember that spending on pharmaceuticals is increasing primarily because more people are relying on new and better medicines, not because prices are increasing.

It is also important to remember that spending on pharmaceuticals still remains a small portion of the health care dollar. Of every health care dollar spent in the U.S., only about 9 cents is spent on prescription medicines. While drug spending continues to grow, it remains a *very small share* of national spending. . . .

Increased spending on pharmaceuticals often leads to lower spending on other forms of more costly health care. New drugs are the most heavily advertised drugs, a point critics often emphasize. However, a new study in *Health Affairs* reports that the use of newer drugs tends to lower all types of non-drug medical spending, resulting in a net reduction in the total cost of treating a condition. An $18 increase in money spent on new prescription drug expenditures reduces non-drug spending by $71.09, resulting in a net savings of $53.09.

Pharmaceutical manufacturers spend far more on research and development (R&D) than on marketing and promotion. In 2001, the research-based pharmaceutical industry R&D:
- Exceeded DTCA spending by over $27.6 billion.
- Exceeded total promotional spending, excluding the value of samples, by over $21.7 billion.
- Exceeded total promotional spending, including the value of samples, by $11.2 billion. . . .

DTCA clearly is here to stay, and will best realize its potential as physicians "develop strategies for helping their patients evaluate this information and make appropriate and informed treatment choices [according to Rosenthal Berndt et al.]." With such a diversity of treatment options available for acute and chronic diseases, patients need the guidance that only a trusted health professional can provide. The health care system is stronger as a consequence. DTCA does not replace that relationship; rather, its purpose is to encourage an informed discussion between patient and physician.

5

Antidepressants May Cause Suicidal Behavior in Youths

Elizabeth Shogren

Elizabeth Shogren, a national correspondent for the Los Angeles Times, *covers environmental issues for its Washington, D.C., bureau. She has also covered the White House, Congress, and social policy.*

Many parents blame the use of antidepressant drugs for their teenagers' suicides. Pressured by the enraged families and some members of Congress, the Food and Drug Administration (FDA) investigated the clinical trials of nine antidepressants and learned that hundreds of youths between the ages of six and eighteen experienced suicidal thoughts while using prescribed antidepressants, though none of them killed themselves. As a result of the continuing studies, FDA advisory panels recommended that the agency warn doctors and families of the risk and add warning labels on antidepressants that the drugs can cause suicidal behavior in youths.

Seven years ago, Mark Miller's 13-year-old son, Matt, who loved to ride bikes and play video games and excelled at making origami animals, hanged himself in his bedroom closet. His parents were devastated—and mystified.

"He had never threatened suicide," Miller recalled. "The only thing that had changed that week in his life was the medication."

Seven days before his death, Matt had begun taking Zoloft, a popular antidepressant prescribed by his doctor.

Antidepressants Come Under Scrutiny

His father, struggling to understand what had happened, dived into the Internet, where he found books on the risks of antidepressants. He was soon convinced that the drug had caused Matt's death.

Miller helped start a website about the risks of the antidepressants. He wrote to the Food and Drug Administration [FDA] and his congressman to enlist the government's help.

At first, no one took him seriously.

There is a risk that antidepressants can cause suicidal behavior in children.

"I always felt people looked at me and said, 'That poor man, he's a bereaved father and he wants to blame it on the medication,'" Miller recalled.

But he gradually found other parents with stories like his. What began as a lonely mission grew into a crusade of about a dozen enraged parents motivated by the belief that their children were ripped from them by the drugs that were supposed to help them.

Finally, the government listened.

Last week [September 2004], two FDA advisory panels recommended that the agency require companies to place prominent warnings—the kind boxed in dark lines—that there is a risk that antidepressants can cause suicidal behavior in children.

Doctors wrote an estimated 15 million prescriptions for nine antidepressants for children and teenagers last year [2003].

Antidepressants May Not Be Safe

Congressional committees are investigating whether the drugs are safe and whether the drug companies or the FDA improperly disguised or underestimated the drugs' risks to children. The FDA will also explore whether the drugs promote suicidal tendencies in adults and violent behavior in patients of all ages.

The FDA recently found that in clinical trials involving nine antidepressants taken by more than 4,000 children ages 6 to 18, hundreds experienced suicidal behavior or thoughts, although none killed themselves.

Miller said he and other parents like him had finally received "vindication and validation of what we've been saying for so long."

For years, as government agencies ignored his pleas, Miller was driven by guilt—he had told his son to take the pills—and sustained by his conversations with people seeking help because their loved ones had become suicidal or violent while taking antidepressants.

"I always thought if I could just reach one more person before his son or daughter did something tragic, it would be worth it. It has become a very bittersweet labor of love," Miller said.

Tom Woodward of suburban Philadelphia found Miller's website, but not until it was too late. When Julie Woodward, 17, was going through a "rough patch" last year, a psychiatrist urged her to take Zoloft, which he assured the family was mild, safe and effective. Seven days later, her father found her body hanging in the garage.

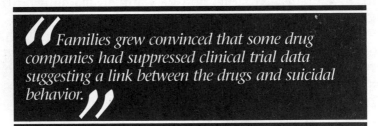

Families grew convinced that some drug companies had suppressed clinical trial data suggesting a link between the drugs and suicidal behavior.

The Woodwards' next-door neighbor, Doug Ross, a neuroscientist, turned to the Internet, where he learned that just a month earlier, the FDA had issued a warning that Paxil, another popular antidepressant, might be linked to increased risk of suicidal thoughts and attempts in young people.

It did not take long, Woodward recalled, before he and his wife were "absolutely convinced that the drug had done this," referring to Julie's death.

The Woodwards found Miller's website, http://www.drug awareness.org/. They had long talks with Miller and other parents about the similar circumstances surrounding their children's deaths.

The families grew convinced that some drug companies

had suppressed clinical trial data suggesting a link between the drugs and suicidal behavior. They resolved to make the government do something.

Today [2004], they regularly share information about new scientific studies and plot strategies to push Congress to act.

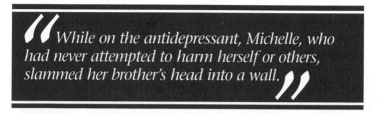

While on the antidepressant, Michelle, who had never attempted to harm herself or others, slammed her brother's head into a wall.

"We've become very, very close to a lot of these other families," Tom Woodward said. "We are bound together by a parent's worst nightmare."

Most of the families met for the first time in person in February [2004] at a hotel bar in Bethesda, Md., where one FDA advisory panel was scheduled to hear their stories the next day.

Antidepressants Need Warning Labels

Their accounts helped persuade the panel to urge the agency to warn doctors and families about the risk of suicide—and of the need to vigilantly monitor patients. But at that point, the FDA stopped short of suggesting that the drugs caused the suicidal behavior.

One of the most tireless members of the parents' group is Lisa Van Syckel of New Jersey, whose daughter, 15-year-old Michelle, was put on Paxil after having been misdiagnosed in 2000 as anorexic and depressed. It turned out that Michelle had Lyme disease.

But while on the antidepressant, Michelle, who had never attempted to harm herself or others, slammed her brother's head into a wall, went after another teenager with a baseball bat and attempted to take her own life. Van Syckel came across Miller's drug awareness website in 2002, as she was trying to ease her daughter off Paxil. Soon she was spending most of her time trying to get someone in power to warn other parents of the dangers of antidepressants. Most political leaders ignored her letters; one exception was Sen. Charles E. Schumer (D-N.Y.), who asked her to join him at a news conference in New York calling on the FDA to discourage the use of Paxil by children.

Then she turned to her own congressman, Rep. Michael Ferguson (R-N.J.). Ferguson became a major force behind a House subcommittee's investigation of the safety of the antidepressants and the role of drug companies and the FDA. "It was [Van Syckel] who really got my attention and prompted me to take an active and leading role," Ferguson said. It was not easy, he said, to get members of Congress to focus on the issue during an election year, when the country was already absorbed by terrorism and the war in Iraq.

But, he said, "we need to investigate this particular issue and get to the bottom of why this is having such an enormous impact on our kids. That cause has been moved forward light-years because of the powerful personal stories of people like Lisa Van Syckel."

Pressure from the families and members of Congress helped prod the FDA to have its advisory committees assess data from clinical trials of children on antidepressants.

Even the drug companies were impressed. "The families had an impact on helping this to move forward," said Dr. Joseph Camardo, medical director for Wyeth Pharmaceuticals North America, which makes one of the popular antidepressants. "I thought it was a great example of how the public can and should be heard."

The families were gratified when the advisory panels recommended last week [September 2004] that the FDA put emphatic warnings on the drugs. Mark Miller, who launched the crusade seven years earlier, called it "a wonderful first step." He added: "I didn't think it would happen in my lifetime."

The parents will continue to press the FDA to extend the warnings to adults and to add a warning that the drugs cause some people to become hostile or even homicidal. They also want Congress to hold the FDA and the drug companies accountable for failing to warn people sooner.

"I can't bear to think of the lives that have been lost in the intervening years," Miller said.

6

Antidepressants Can Help Despondent Teens

Nancy Shute

Nancy Shute is a science writer for U.S. News & World Report.

Many teenagers suffer from depression; every year approximately 20 percent of adolescents contemplate suicide, and of these, one out of every ten attempts suicide by the end of high school. A 2004 study showed that the antidepressant Prozac can significantly reduce feelings of hopelessness, isolation, and irritability. Although there has been much publicity about the risk of suicide for young people taking antidepressants, parents should not be deterred from seeking treatment—including the use of antidepressants—to help their depressed children. Untreated depression is a greater risk than the use of antidepressants.

W alk into any high school classroom in the country today, and chances are at least one student there is suffering from a debilitating illness called depression. But when parents seek help for their children, they all too often find themselves frustrated by a lack of information on how best to treat the psychiatric disorder. Despite the high rate of depression in kids, remedies have for the most part been untested, so families of these kids have been left to grope in the dark.

Last week [August 2004] the darkness lifted a bit, when researchers made public the results of the first study to compare depression treatments in teenagers. The headline of their work:

Nearly 3 in 4 of their young patients improved significantly with a combination of psychotherapy and Prozac, a popular brand of the antidepressant drug class known as SSRIs [selective serotonin reuptake inhibitors]. Of the 439 teens who participated in the nationwide study, 61 percent of those receiving Prozac alone got better after 12 weeks of treatment.

Study Proves Treatment Successful

Psychiatrists widely praised the findings as long-overdue and much-needed evidence in the confusing and increasingly controversial realm of depression treatment. The study is also an all-too-rare application of the controls that are standard in nonpsychiatric medical trials, in which participants are randomly assigned to different treatments and neither they nor their physicians know if they'e getting the medication being tested or a dummy pill. "We now have solid clinical evidence that we can help kids significantly—and pretty quickly," says David Fassler, a child and adolescent psychiatrist in Burlington, Vt. "I think parents and physicians should be reassured."

We now have solid clinical evidence that we can help kids significantly.

Patient advocates also welcomed the findings. "It should take a lot of fear away from families," says Lydia Lewis, president of the Depression and Bipolar Support Alliance in Chicago. "The whole deal of patient empowerment is knowledge. You can't know if you're getting good treatment unless you know what good treatment is." The teenagers who received the combination treatment got 15 sessions of cognitive-behavioral therapy, a widely used form of psychotherapy that focuses on recasting the negative thoughts typical of depression and increasing positive thoughts and actions. Sessions with parents and other family members were included. Previous studies have shown cognitive-behavioral therapy alone to be very effective in treating depression in adolescents, with about 60 percent showing improvement. But in this case, talk therapy alone helped just 43 percent of the time, a number not much different from the 35 percent who improved while taking placebo pills. John March, a child psychiatrist at Duke University Medical Center and lead researcher for the Treatment for Adolescents With Depression Study (known as TADS), whose results were published in last week's [August 2004] *Journal of the American Medical Association*, says the poor response to talk therapy may reflect the fact that the study included only patients with moderate to severe depression and that most study participants had been depressed for about a year.

Antidepressants Are Beneficial Despite Suicide Risks

The TADS research is also significant because it is one of the very few studies of antidepressants that were not financed by a drug manufacturer; instead, backing came from the National Institute of Mental Health. Antidepressants have come under increased scrutiny in the past year after it was revealed that pharmaceutical companies have failed to publish data suggesting increased rates of suicide in people taking SSRI antidepressants, the most commonly used form of the drugs. Teenagers and adults in their early 20s are far more likely to commit suicide than older adults. Each year, about 20 percent of adolescents contemplate suicide; by the end of high school, 1 in 10 of those has attempted suicide, with almost 2,000 succeeding each year. Half of those who die had major clinical depression, which is characterized by feelings of hopelessness, isolation, and irritability. What's to blame? Psychiatrists have long known that some people become agitated, anxious, and have trouble sleeping when they start taking SSRIs. The speculation is that this "activation" may make patients more apt to injure themselves or others, because the drug has lessened the despair and lassitude typical of depression. But there are no reliable data available to support this theory. And because suicide is an outcome of the condition that the drugs are supposed to treat, it's difficult to sort out whether the disease or the treatment is at fault.

Prozac (generic name fluoxetine), the drug used in the TADS study, is the only SSRI antidepressant approved by the Food and Drug Administration for use in children. But physicians frequently prescribe other SSRIs, which include Zoloft, Paxil, and Effexor, to children "off label," a practice allowed by the FDA. Thus, there is intense interest in finding out whether all SSRIs increase the risk of suicide or whether some may pose more of a risk than others.

Last year [2003], the FDA's British counterpart, citing un-published data, banned the use of SSRIs—aside from Prozac—for children. In March [2004], the FDA ordered antidepressant manufacturers to add warning labels urging physicians to watch patients closely for worsening depression and suicidal tendencies. . . .

Last week's [August 2004] report doesn't answer the suicide question, because it followed too few participants over too short a time to detect trends. March's group is continuing the TADS study and is also launching a second study of SSRI use in 1,600 children that he hopes will provide some answers. But the TADS data do show that, while suicidal thoughts were reduced from 29 percent to 10 percent for all study participants, those taking Prozac were slightly more likely to harm themselves or others. Cognitive-behavioral therapy, both alone and with Prozac, ap-peared to have a protective effect. March and other psychiatrists say this points out the importance of carefully monitoring any patient given antidepressants, particularly in the first weeks. "Hopefully, this trial will do away with the idea that any kid who takes SSRIs will get psychotic mania and kill themselves," March says.

Indeed, although psychiatrists say more research on the safety of SSRIs is urgently needed, they also fear that the in-creased publicity on potential risks may frighten parents away from seeking help for their children. Untreated depression, they contend, is far more likely to result in suicide. Already, 80 percent of children with mental illness in the United States aren't getting any treatment, according to the surgeon general, and parents who do seek help for their children often find themselves thwarted by insurers who don't cover mental-health care and by a lack of qualified therapists. "It might take some moxie to get your kid to the head of the line, because mental-health care is pretty severely rationed in this country," says Ken Duckworth, a child psychiatrist and medical director for the National Alliance for the Mentally Ill. "But the biggest risk is to do nothing."

7

Importing Drugs from Canada Is Dangerous

Peter Pitts

Peter Pitts was formerly an associate commissioner for external relations at the U.S. Food and Drug Administration. He is now a senior fellow in health care studies at the Pacific Research Institute.

High prescription drug costs have become a serious problem for many Americans, especially seniors who live on fixed incomes. People desperate for a solution are eager to legalize the widespread importation of pharmaceuticals from Canada and other foreign countries where government-imposed price controls keep the costs of prescription drugs lower than in the United States. However, legalization would create many problems, including an increase in the threat of counterfeit drugs and the risk that terrorists could contaminate drugs to kill Americans. Canada has stated that it cannot monitor the shipment of drugs across the U.S. border, and the U.S. Food and Drug Administration has already discovered Canadian companies selling fake and contaminated versions of prescription medicines. Instead of seeking out Canadian drugs, American consumers who need to decrease their health care expenses should check with their doctors to see if generic versions of brand-name prescriptions are available.

When it comes to medicines, Americans historically have been attracted to offers of quick, easy cures.

In the late 19th and early 20th centuries, those offers were the core of the so-called "patent medicine" industry, with innumerable shysters peddling panaceas. Today's cable TV spots for Viagra are models of restraint compared to the newspaper ads of a hundred years ago for patent medicines promising cures for everything from depression to diarrhea.

Most of the cures were useless. Some were harmless, others were downright dangerous. They might provide some temporary relief from pain or restore your energy, but the core ingredients that did the job were alcohol, cocaine, and opium.

Americans Want Lower Drug Prices

Eventually, of course, the frauds of the patent medicine world were exposed, leading Congress to pass the Pure Food and Drug Act of 1906. But don't get the idea that we've been cured of our traditional weakness for quick easy "cures" in matters of health care. That weakness is very much in evidence as America wrestles with the chronic issue of prescription drug costs. And the quick, easy cure of choice these days seems to come down to two words: drug imports.

Our appetite for a solution is understandable. Drug costs in America are a high-value bargain compared to the cost of hospitalization modern drugs avoid. Because of advanced pharmaceuticals, we are living longer and more productive lives.

But individual drug costs are high, especially for seniors living on Social Security and the vagaries of a shaky investment income. Since seniors are by far the biggest users of prescription drugs, monthly pharmacy bills of $300 and $400 a month are not uncommon.

Many well-intentioned people, some of them public officials, believe that the key to containing drug costs in the U.S. is to legalize and encourage the widespread importing of drugs from foreign countries where government-imposed price controls allow the sale of drugs at prices lower than those charged for name-brand drugs in a U.S. pharmacy.

Importing Drugs Is Gambling with Safety

But like the addictive patent medicines of a hundred years ago, widespread drug imports would create more problems than they would solve. The number-one problem would be a massive threat to public health caused by a flood of imported drugs not subject to quality control and monitoring by anyone.

Counterfeit drugs are already a huge global problem, especially in developing nations. According to some experts, as much as $50 billion worth of the $500 billion in international drug sales each year is made in counterfeit drugs.

With the global supply of counterfeit drugs huge and growing, it's obvious that the U.S. drug market—which accounts for fully half of the world's medicine sales—would be a prime target for counterfeiters if we make their job easy by weakening our current drug import protections. And unfortunately, it's also a fact of life that massive drug imports would create a major opportunity for international terrorists to kill thousands of Americans with intentionally contaminated drugs packaged as legitimate pharmaceuticals.

For the better part of the last hundred years, Americans have been able to go to their pharmacy and buy pills or liquids and be totally confident that the medicine in the container is exactly what the doctor prescribed. That's a comfort level we've come to take for granted, but it will be gone if imports put us in a position of depending on drugs of uncertain origin, produced and stored under conditions beyond our control.

Widespread drug imports would create more problems than they would solve.

And that applies to drugs imported from Canada, our friendly neighbor to the north. U.S. advocates of drug imports like to suggest special importing arrangements with Canada because, to the chagrin of Canadians, many Americans think of Canada as just a cold extension of the USA. Most of the people speak English. It's a stable democracy with a legal system very much like ours and a national health agency that guards the purity of drugs sold in Canada just as aggressively as the FDA does in the States.

Canada Cannot Monitor Drug Shipments

True enough, but none of that guarantees the safety of drug exports from Canada to the U.S.—and nobody is more adamant about that than the Canadians themselves. The country's national health agency, Health Canada, has been up-front about saying they cannot possibly monitor drug shipments across the U.S. border. That's because many of those drugs aren't even produced in Canada.

Through a process known as "transshipment," drugs come into Canada from around the world, including developing countries like China, Chile, India, Belize, the Bahamas and Vietnam. Most of these third-country drugs are mailed to customers in the U.S. from the growing number of Internet pharmacies in Canada that take prescriptions from Americans, sometimes with the help of Canadian physicians hired to write prescriptions.

Massive drug imports would create a major opportunity for international terrorists to kill thousands of Americans.

While Canada's pharmacy standards are close to ours, there's always a greater chance for misunderstanding or outright deception when something as important as a personal prescription is handled over the Internet. That chance was underscored in July of 2004 when the FDA found that a Canadian website pharmacy advertising Canadian generic drugs was in fact selling fake, contaminated and substandard versions of three widely prescribed medicines.

Even if the quality of drug imports were not in question, having Canada supply the U.S. with prescriptions is a bad deal economically for both countries and provides very little in the way of actual savings for consumers.

Importation Is Not the Answer

A detailed report on drug imports issued last year [2004] by the U.S. Department of Health and Human Services [HHS] estimated that total savings to U.S. consumers from legalized commercial importation of drugs would be only one to two percent of total drug spending. The HHS pointed out that most of the price difference between U.S. and imported drugs would go to third-party payers such as insurance companies and HMOs.

And in the government-controlled health market of Canada, the supply of legitimate drugs sold in each province is sharply rationed. Diverting more and more of this limited supply for sale to Americans is aggravating a shortage of some drugs. No wonder the Health Minister of Canada recently warned that "Canada cannot be the drugstore of the United States." Canada's government appears to be looking to shut down transshipment of drugs, anyway. So even if it were a good idea, it won't last.

It's pretty clear that drug imports from Canada or anywhere else are not a viable, long-term solution for easing the cost of prescription drugs for Americans. But there are more options open than ever before, especially for senior citizens, and they don't carry the health risks of imports.

The HHS study on drug imports reported that average prices for generic drugs in the U.S. are 50 percent lower than they are in foreign countries. That's right—American generics are cheaper than Canadian generics. So consumers of all ages should check with their doctor or pharmacist for a generic version available as a substitute for brand-name prescriptions.

People in a financial bind over paying for prescription drugs can also get help directly from the pharmaceutical companies. Each major company in the U.S. has a patient-assistance program that is easy to access and provides free or significantly discounted medications. In 2003 these programs filled over 18 million prescriptions a year at no cost.

For seniors, of course, there are the new Medicare drug discount cards. Any senior can enroll and be eligible for drug discounts ranging from 10 to 75 percent on prescription drugs. Low-income seniors are entitled to $600 in medicines for 2005 under the drug card program, in addition to the discounts.

The discount cards are an interim step until the full Medicare prescription drug benefit program kicks in in 2006. Seniors and the people who care about them have been waiting for a Medicare drug benefit since the original program was created back in 1965. Its protection against catastrophic drug costs alone will guarantee that no senior is ever again made destitute by the drug demands of a serious illness.

That sounds like a good solution to me. And in the tradition of good solutions, it didn't come quick and it didn't come easy.

8

Importing Drugs from Canada Is Safe

Josh Fischman

Josh Fischman is a staff writer for U.S. News & World Report.

The price of prescription drugs has become prohibitive for many Americans, threatening the health of those who cannot afford needed drugs. To address this problem, several state governors and city mayors have initiated programs to help consumers buy cheaper medicine from Canada. Although the Food and Drug Administration (FDA) claims that pharmaceuticals imported from Canada could be counterfeit or tainted, the drugs can be safe and economical provided certain precautions are followed. Some of the state programs have inspected the Canadian pharmacies they do business with in order to check their safety practices. In addition, a study by the U.S. government of eighteen Canadian Internet pharmacies found that none sold fake or counterfeit drugs. Nonetheless, consumers should be careful about ordering pharmaceuticals that are not vetted by state programs.

The half-dozen elderly people meeting at Horseshoe Pond Place, an independent living facility in Concord, N.H., were, for once, impressed with a government initiative. In their quest to afford the drugs that, in many cases, keep them alive, they had tried to sort through assistance programs offered by pharmaceutical companies and the new Medicare discount cards, all in a pricing landscape that changes from one day to the next. But when Gov. Craig Benson came to Horseshoe Pond to explain the state's website with links to Canadian pharmacies, Virginia North, 77, voiced approval. "He asked us to throw out the names of drugs we used. I said Lopid." She takes the heart drug to reduce her triglyceride levels. "I pay $150 for 90 days. Through this Internet, I could get it for $50 for 90 days. I think that's great," she says.

Political Leaders Get Involved

Benson is one of seven governors, along with mayors from cities such as Springfield, Mass., and Columbia, S.C., who have kicked off or announced programs in the past year [2004] that make it easy to get cheaper medicine from Canada, where price controls keep costs low. "I can't tell you how many seniors I've met who simply cannot afford their drugs," says Benson. And it's not just seniors but young people and new parents and working, middle-aged couples. Many New Hampshire residents used to ride buses across the border to fill their prescriptions. "Why should we make old people sit on buses for three or four hours, when they can do it through the Internet where it's easier and safer?" Benson asks.

Because it isn't safer, answers the FDA [Food and Drug Administration]; in fact it is downright dangerous. "You can not only lose your money but also your health," says William Hubbard, the FDA's associate commissioner for policy and planning. Drugs from Internet pharmacies, even those in nice, safe Canada, could be counterfeit, tainted, mislabeled, and unapproved. And Hubbard and others worry that the state programs remove such drugs from FDA inspection. "Apparently these pharmacies will sell you anything," Hubbard says. "And once you tell the FDA to get out of the way, it's 'Katy, bar the door!'"

There Are Risks, but Also Safeguards

Is this literally a case of your money or your life? Must people choose between safe drugs and affordable drugs? Not really. There are some risks, but it turns out there are also steps careful consumers can—and should—take to safeguard both wallet and health. Choose Canadian pharmacies wisely: Some of the state programs have actually sent inspectors to specific pharmacies to check their supply and their practices for safety. You should also be careful about the medications you request, using the Canadian sites for refills only after you and your U.S. doctor know how the drugs affect you. "I think our website has stepped in to provide people with quality assurances," says Kevin Goodno, commissioner of human services in Minnesota, which runs an importation program. "We feel the pharmacies we use meet or even exceed the standards of Minnesota pharmacies." Adds Scott McKibbin, who helped design the Illinois plan, set to kick off by the end of the month [September 2004]: "Myself, my wife, and our four kids will be in this program. So there's no way I'm compromising on safety."

McKibbin, Goodno, and others began looking across the border as prescription drug prices soared in this country, rising much faster than the rate of inflation. The average cost of widely used brand-name drugs went from $33.76 in 2000 to $60.38 in 2003, according to a study by the AARP [American Association of Retired Persons] Public Policy Institute. "So what you see is sick people choosing not to buy drugs, and in my view that's the real health risk here," says Goodno. "We felt we had to do something."

> *There are some risks [in importing drugs from Canada], but . . . there are also steps careful consumers can—and should—take to safeguard both wallet and health.*

That something turned out to be Canadian imports, which were attractive for two reasons. First, the Canadian government has a national healthcare system that sets drug prices, which can be 70 percent lower than in the United States. Second, the Canadian drug-safety system mirrors that of the United States, with a federal agency—Health Canada—regulating drugs based on therapeutic value and good manufacturing standards, and with local pharmacy boards licensing and inspecting all pharmacies.

Plus, while the U.S. government has been adamant about keeping American drugs under FDA oversight, blocking all unapproved imports, the agency—so far—has interpreted the law to allow a "personal use" exemption, which means a person with a valid U.S. prescription from a doctor can bring in up to a 90-day supply of a drug.

Minnesota was the first state to put all these elements together. It sent a team of pharmacy inspectors to Canada who looked at the credentials, licensing, suppliers, and volume capacity of eight pharmacies interested in selling to the American public. The state selected two of these pharmacies for a site, *minnesotarxconnect.com*, that launched early this year [2004]: Total Care Pharmacy in Calgary and Granville Pharmacy in Vancouver. (Two more pharmacies were added this spring [2004].)

At the site, consumers are provided a list of drugs and advised to order only refills and not to order narcotics. They download an application in which they list their complete medical history and attach a valid U.S. prescription, and fax it to the pharmacy. The pharmacy forwards the information to a Canadian physician for review, and the doctor then writes it up as a Canadian prescription (U.S. prescriptions are not valid in Canada). Payment is usually by credit card, and in two to three weeks the customer gets a 90-day supply of the drug. Insurance companies generally reimburse for the drugs as they would for U.S. prescriptions.

Wisconsin, after its own inspections, soon followed with a similar system (*drugsavings.wi.gov*) with similar requirements for both consumers and drugstores. North Dakota and New Hampshire also added websites, which link directly to the Canadian stores, which have their own patient information forms. A few cities, such as Columbia, S.C., and Washington, D.C., have added "tagalong" links to city web pages that direct consumers to the state sites. (Springfield, Mass., has gone even further and contracted with a Canadian drug clearinghouse to supply specific drugs to city employees and retirees.)

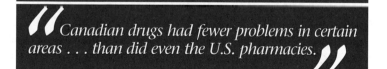

Canadian drugs had fewer problems in certain areas . . . than did even the U.S. pharmacies.

All this due diligence sounds good on paper, say Hubbard and other critics, but in reality the programs have serious holes. "The big problem is that Canada can't supply all these drugs from legitimate sources," says Marvin Shepherd, director of the pharmacoeconomics center at the University of Texas–Austin. The country has a small population, and drug companies such as Pfizer and GlaxoSmithKline limit what they send north of the border. Pharmacies are thought to turn to sources like China, Israel, and Mexico to fill American orders. "We don't really know the pedigree of these drugs," says Tom McGinnis, FDA's director of pharmacy affairs. Druggists may think they are getting the real deal from their wholesalers and distributors, but the products may be manufactured badly or not equivalent to FDA-approved medications. Indeed, Hubbard listed 15 violations of good pharmacy practice that turned up in Minnesota's own inspections and noted that Wisconsin's Canadian partners shipped unapproved drugs in violation of their contract with the state.

Canada Practices Due Diligence

That sounds worrisome. But Goodno points out that of Hubbard's 15 violations, 12 applied to the pharmacies Minnesota rejected, not to the four they actually partnered with. As for unapproved drugs sent to Wisconsin, Sue Reinardy of the state health department says they were generics approved but not yet available in the United States, and the ban on them wasn't clear in the contracts; pharmacies stopped sending them as soon as this was clarified. "This actually contradicts the FDA objections that we're out of control," says Dave Robertson, president of Calgary's Total Care. "As soon as they told us to stop, we stopped."

But what about counterfeit or faulty products? It doesn't appear to be a real Canadian problem. This spring [2004], the Government Accountability Office [GAO], the investigative arm of Congress, ordered 11 different drugs from more than 60 different Internet pharmacies, including 18 Canadian ones. The GAO sent the medicines—such as the cholesterol drug Lipitor and the arthritis drug Celebrex—back to the original manufacturers to check their chemistry and activity. "In other words, we asked them to tell us if this was indeed their drug," says Marcia Crosse, who directed the study. None of the drugs from Canada were fakes. And the Canadian drugs had fewer problems in certain areas (specifically improper shipping or no pharmacy label attached to prescriptions) than did even the U.S. pharmacies. "I don't think you can say, based on our small sample, that it's absolutely safe," says Crosse. "But we certainly felt more comfortable with Canada."

To increase your comfort level, if you decide to go the Canadian route, it would be wise to take several steps. The FDA isn't wrong: There are bad guys out there. So deal with the pharmacies already vetted by states; you don't have to be a state resident to use these websites. Try a new drug first from a U.S. pharmacy, to check for side effects, and then use the Canadian pharmacy for refills. Don't order anything that needs to be refrigerated, like insulin, because you never know what will happen during shipping. And compare labels with your U.S. prescription. If the directions are not the same—and some Canadian labeling requirements are different—check with your doctor before using the drug. Don't order Canadian generics; because there's more generic drug competition in the United States, driving prices down, American generics are usually cheaper.

Cheaper and safer drugs, after all, is what this is all about.

9

The Food and Drug Administration Promotes Dangerous Prescription Drugs

Mike Adams

Mike Adams is a writer for the News Target Web site. His stated mission is to provide information that can improve the lives of people everywhere.

The U.S. Food and Drug Administration (FDA) was originally created to protect the public health. However, growing evidence shows that the FDA has approved and promoted dangerous prescription drugs in order to protect the financial interests of pharmaceutical companies. For example, the FDA allowed the painkiller Vioxx to be sold to the American public even though it knew the drug could increase the risk of heart attacks. The FDA also censors its own scientists in order to prevent them from testifying about the dangers of drugs such as antidepressants. The FDA's well-publicized criminal behavior has destroyed the public trust in the federal agency, which will need to be completely revamped to end its corruption and restore its reputation.

The reputation of both the FDA [Food Drug Administration] and Merck [pharmaceutical company] lies in shambles today [2005] after evidence continues to surface that shows the FDA knowingly approved, promoted and refused to recall a dangerous drug that caused tens of thousands of fatalities among the American population: Vioxx [a painkiller]. The FDA sees its job as promoting drugs and the financial interests of pharmaceutical companies, not as protecting the public health. We've known, all along, that it would take a scandal to reveal the true nature of the FDA and see serious calls for reform. Well, folks, the scandal is here, and the FDA is now under intense fire by the international medical community for its role in covering up the truth about Vioxx for four years.

Criticism of the FDA

Perhaps the most relevant criticism of the agency comes from Dr. Richard Horton, editor of *The Lancet,* a well respected medical journal. After reading the Merck insider emails published in the *Wall Street Journal* showing how Merck sought to distort drug trials to hide evidence of heart disease, and after reviewing the same clinical trials on the drug that the FDA reviewed before approving it, Dr. Horton was outraged and described the agency's senior management as ". . . more concerned with external appearance than rigorous science."

He continued with: "In the case of Vioxx, the FDA was urged to mandate further clinical safety testing after a 2001 analysis suggested a 'clear-cut excess number of myocardial infarctions'. It did not do so. This refusal to engage with an issue of grave clinical concern illustrates the agency's in-built paralysis, a predicament that has to be addressed through fundamental organizational reform."

> *The FDA knowingly approved, promoted and refused to recall a dangerous drug that caused tens of thousands of fatalities among the American population.*

But Dr. Horton didn't stop there. He also explained, ". . . with Vioxx, Merck and the FDA acted out of ruthless, short-sighted, and irresponsible self-interest." In other words, Merck and the FDA were playing the classic "cover your ass" game in trying to hide the destructive health consequences of Vioxx from the public for as long as possible. And they managed to pull it off for four years thanks to the gullibility of conventional doctors and the ignorance of the American public, who continue to believe in prescription drugs as "miracle cures" for just about every symptom or disease, even though the facts reveal that prescription drugs heal no one. As we're now learning, prescription drugs actually harm or kill people.

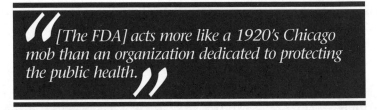

[The FDA] acts more like a 1920's Chicago mob than an organization dedicated to protecting the public health.

For example, antidepressants now carry warnings about causing birth defects. The same drugs are also known to cause violent behavior in children. Statin drugs cause brain fog and interfere with vitamin D production, calcium absorption and libido. And anti-inflammatory drugs cause heart attacks and strokes. These destructive side effects are only now coming to light after years of suppression and denial by drug companies and the FDA. What kind of suppression? On antidepressant drugs, for example, major drug companies sent warning letters to doctors in the U.K. about the links between antidepressant drugs and suicidal behavior, but refused to go public with the same warning in the United States.

The FDA Does Not Protect the Public

For decades, the public has blindingly trusted the FDA, despite the growing evidence that the agency acts more like a 1920's Chicago mob than an organization dedicated to protecting the public health. The FDA is far more interested in protecting the profits of Big Pharma [major pharmaceutical companies], it seems. In a very real sense, the FDA is the godfather of the U.S. drug racket, where dangerous chemicals are hyped, approved and sold to the American people, regardless of their true dangers. I've been shouting this message for years, and now, finally, people around the world are starting to listen. Even the FDA's own scientists, when given the opportunity to tell the truth about the agency, have nothing but criticism. Dr. David Graham, a veteran drug safety researcher at the FDA, said flatly, "I would argue that the FDA as currently configured is incapable of protecting America against another Vioxx."

He went on to say, ". . . the FDA is not able to adequately protect the American public. It's more interested in protecting the interests of industry. It views industry as its client, and the client is someone whose interest you represent. . . . The structural problems that exist within the FDA, where the people who approve the drugs are also the ones who oversee the post marketing regulation of the drug, remain unchanged. The people who approve a drug when they see that there is a safety problem with it are very reluctant to do anything about it because it will reflect badly on them."

> *In a sane world, the FBI would march into the FDA offices tomorrow and arrest these white-collar hucksters for the crimes they have committed.*

The FDA, by the way, attempted to silence Dr. David Graham and prevent him from testifying before Congress about the dangers of prescription drugs. This is one small example of the FDA's ongoing campaign of suppression and censorship designed to keep the American people in the dark about the true dangers of prescription drugs while protecting the profits of drug companies.

The FDA Censors Its Own Scientists

Another FDA researcher, Dr. Andrew Mosholder, was censored and not allowed to testify in February, 2004 about his study that found antidepressants increase the risk of suicides in children. There was a war within the FDA between the scientists who recognized the clear health risks of drugs like Prozac and Vioxx, vs. the top administrators who wanted to keep pushing drugs to the public regardless of their health risk. As Dr. David Graham explained, "the review and clearance process had been turned into a battleground, full of contention and intimidation because our managers, the people who fill out our performance evaluations, had created a system where it was taking a great risk to stand firm in our scientific beliefs."

That's how the FDA operates: censor any scientists who speak out against prescription drugs. Delay the bad news, keep dangerous drugs on the market as long as possible, and keep the profit machine pumping for Big Pharma. (Read the story about Rezulin, the diabetes drug, if you want to learn some real dirt on how this drug profit machine really operates.)

Today, the FDA's reputation is in shambles. Finally, the world is getting the picture: the agency cannot be trusted. It has now proven, yet again, that it will co-conspire with drug companies to distort the truth, lie to the American public, and blatantly promote dangerous drugs that it knows are killing people.

Blatant Criminal Behavior at the FDA

These actions are not mere "administrative oversight," folks. These actions represent a pattern of criminal behavior on the part of FDA employees and drug company executives. Promoting these toxic drugs, distorting the clinical trials, and burying the negative evidence are criminal actions and should be treated as such. In a sane world, the FBI would march into the FDA offices tomorrow and arrest these white-collar hucksters for the crimes they have committed. In my opinion, executives at Merck should do prison time—plus pay billions in fines—for the pain, suffering and death they have unleashed upon the population.

Quite clearly, Big Pharma is a highly corrupt industry, and it is backed and promoted by a federal agency that needs to be wiped clean and rebuilt from scratch (along with a new office of Internal Affairs that would investigate FDA employees for precisely these sort of crimes).

Regardless of what happens next, it's evident that the public trust in the FDA has been destroyed. ". . . the most important legacy of this episode," writes Dr. Horton, "is the continued erosion of trust that public-health institutions will suffer. Failure to act decisively on signals of risk might minimize short-term political criticism for regulators, or shareholder unrest for company chief executives. But the long-term consequence of prevarication is a tide of public skepticism about just whose interests drug makers and regulators truly represent."

That's a very polite way of saying the FDA is in bed with the drug companies—a fact that's as obvious as the fingers on your hand to anyone who has actually been following the FDA's actions over the last few years. There's no question about it: the FDA knowingly and willingly places the financial interests of Big Pharma as its highest priority. And in doing so, it is causing the needless death and suffering of American citizens.

By any definition, that is criminal.

10

The Food and Drug Administration Protects Consumers

Michelle Meadows

Michelle Meadows is a writer and editor for the U.S. Food and Drug Administration.

The mission of the U.S. Food and Drug Administration (FDA) is to ensure that drugs marketed to the public, including prescription drugs, are safe and effective. Even after they have been approved for marketing, prescription drugs continue to be monitored to identify problems that were not observed during clinical drug trials. Also, drug companies are required to inform the FDA of any report of serious adverse reaction not already listed in a drug's labeling. If new risks are found, the FDA demands that those risks be added to the drug's labeling. Every drug involves risks; however, the ultimate question is whether the benefits outweigh those risks. If the FDA believes they do not, it will ask the manufacturer to withdraw the drug.

"But aren't drugs supposed to be safe?" According to Janet Woodcock, M.D., director of the Food and Drug Administration's [FDA] Center for Drug Evaluation and Research (CDER), people tend to ask that question a lot when a drug is taken off the market. The FDA's mission is making sure that drugs are "safe and effective." So what does "safe" really mean?

Michelle Meadows, "Why Drugs Get Pulled Off the Market," *FDA Consumer Magazine*, January/February 2002. Reproduced by permission.

When it comes to any drug, "safe" means that the benefits of the drug outweigh the risks for the population the drug is intended to treat and for its intended use. "Safe does not mean harmless," Woodcock says. "Every drug comes with risks, and our tolerance for risk is higher for drugs that treat serious and life-threatening illnesses. There is no question that cancer drugs can be highly toxic. But they also save lives."

Constant Evaluation

If the FDA decides that a drug's benefits outweigh its risks, the agency approves the drug for marketing. Approved drugs continue to be evaluated through postmarketing surveillance—a system that monitors a drug's safety on an ongoing basis. Postmarketing surveillance seeks to identify problems that weren't observed or recognized before approval and any problems that might arise because a product isn't being used as anticipated.

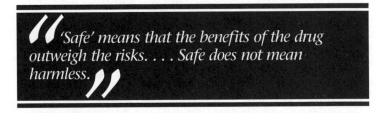

'Safe' means that the benefits of the drug outweigh the risks. . . . Safe does not mean harmless.

The goal is to catch any bad news right away so that the FDA and drug companies can act quickly and communicate new risk information to consumers and doctors. CDER evaluates required reports from drug companies, which must promptly pass on any report they receive of a serious adverse reaction that isn't already described in the drug's labeling. CDER also relies on MedWatch, the system through which consumers and health professionals voluntarily report adverse events associated with all products the FDA regulates.

When the FDA receives reports of significant new adverse events, the agency evaluates them for their seriousness and the likelihood that they were caused by the drug. To the extent possible, the agency also considers how the toxicity compares with other treatments for the same disease. Ultimately, of course, the critical question is: Do the benefits of this drug still outweigh its risks for the population described in the labeling? In many cases, that question cannot be answered immediately, and more reports must be considered. Sometimes, the impact of labeling revisions needs to be assessed.

Usually, when important new risks are uncovered, the risks are added to the drug's labeling and doctors are informed of the new information through letters and other education. It's only rarely that the approval decision on a drug needs to be reassessed and changed. A conclusion that a drug should no longer be marketed is based on the nature and frequency of the adverse effect and how the drug compares with treatment alternatives.

When the FDA believes it is clear that a drug no longer has a place in treatment, it will ask the manufacturer to withdraw the drug voluntarily. Companies have agreed to withdraw the drug in all cases except one—the case of an antidiabetic drug called phenformin, which was taken off the market in 1976 as an imminent hazard, despite the company's objections. If a company does not agree, the FDA can bring formal procedures to require withdrawal.

At first glance, one might assume that every time a drug comes off the market, it means that somewhere along the way somebody made a horrible mistake—that the drug never should have been on the market in the first place. But FDA experts say that would not be correct. Most often, the withdrawal occurs because of adverse effects that were not seen prior to marketing. Sometimes, there was no clue at all. In other cases, one can see hints of the problem in retrospect, but not the serious events that eventually led to the withdrawal.

Many complex factors go into making judgments about benefits and risks, and into ultimately deciding whether a drug should be taken off the market. Here are some major issues, often overlapping, that weigh into the decision-making process.

Rare, Unpredictable Problems

Most drugs on the market are well-tolerated and their adverse effects are known. Known side effects cause more injuries and deaths than unrecognized side effects. But some problems happen so infrequently that they can't be seen or predicted before a drug gets on the market. Serious drug-induced liver disease, for example, is the leading single reason drugs have been pulled from the market. But it is rare, occurring at a rate of 1 in 5,000 to 1 in 10,000 exposures or less. This will not show up in clinical trials, which will pick up relatively common problems.

"If we want reasonably rapid access to needed drugs, it's not practical to require that they be tested in 15,000 to 30,000 people, which is what you'd need to be reasonably sure you saw even one case that occurs at a rate of 1 in 5,000 to 10,000," according to Robert Temple, M.D., director of the FDA's office of medical policy. "And the case would need to be recognized as drug induced," he says. So drugs are typically tested in several thousand subjects, allowing detection of relatively common serious adverse events, such as those affecting 1 in 1,000 people. This practical size of clinical trials means we can't know everything about a drug when it gets on the market. Rare events will only surface when the drug is used in larger numbers of people. Temple says, "Sometimes less severe events that are seen in trials can be used to predict the occurrence of rare, more serious events, but that is not always the case, and such predictions have considerable uncertainty."

The number of subjects in clinical trials is increasing in some areas of drug development, says Peter Honig, M.D., director of the FDA's office of drug safety. "But the numbers will never be large enough to eliminate the need for postmarketing surveillance." The FDA is working on ways to better predict rare events, especially those related to the liver and heart. But some uncertainties will always be there, including the possibility of rare characteristics that make some people particularly susceptible to an adverse reaction. . . .

Accurate Labeling and Warnings

The term "safe" also depends on whether a drug is used according to the labeling. This is why the FDA makes sure labeling and advertising for prescription drugs are accurate and balanced—presenting both the benefits and the risks.

The major problem with Duract (bromfenac), a nonsteroidal anti-inflammatory drug, was that the directions were not followed. The pain drug was withdrawn in 1998 after liver failure occurred in patients who took the short-term treatment for pain for more than the 10 days recommended in the labeling. Clinical trials indicated that a higher incidence of elevated liver enzymes was associated with longer use. Duract's manufacturer, Wyeth-Ayerst Laboratories, Philadephia, added a new warning to the labeling and sent letters out to doctors, but reports of long-term use of the drug continued. . . .

The day you hear news about a drug coming off the market, it may appear to be a sudden, drastic step. But several other options to manage risks usually have been attempted before that point. The main risk management tools employed by the FDA are education through letters to health-care professionals (known within the FDA as "Dear Doctor" letters) and labeling changes, such as new warnings, sometimes boxed in black for emphasis. Also used are required Medication Guides, labeling specifically for patients that emphasizes significant risks and advises patients how to detect or avoid them. In some cases, a drug is labeled as "second line," meaning it is to be used only in patients for whom other treatments fail. In other cases, a drug that is known to be dangerous is still made available under certain circumstances through what's known as restricted distribution.

> *The FDA makes sure labeling and advertising for prescription drugs are accurate and balanced—presenting both the benefits and the risks.*

Sometimes these risk management techniques are effective, and other times they aren't. "We have our anecdotes, but there is little systematic study on the effect of drug labeling changes on physician behavior," says Temple.

Labeling changes were a partial success with the allergy drug Seldane. Studies showed use of Seldane with inappropriate drugs declined almost 90 percent, but that left considerable exposure to the dangerous combinations, some of which could be lethal.

The label of the heartburn treatment Propulsid (cisapride) was changed several times in 1998. The FDA cosponsored a study to evaluate the effect of various regulatory actions, and found that the percentage of patients inappropriately exposed to the drug was unchanged.

"We know that the farther out we are from the initial approval, the less likely we are to change behavior," Woodcock says. "Once a prescribing pattern has been established, it's hard to change it."

Drug Safety Requires Everyone's Involvement

Clearly, the more special care that is required, the more physicians must remember, and the more we need other safeguards like spotting dangerous combination uses at the pharmacy level, the more of a challenge risk management becomes. "We do consider whether we are being unreasonable in our expectations, but sometimes that can't be known beforehand," Temple says.

Currently, the FDA is involved with several drug safety initiatives, including revamping the drug labeling for physicians to create a highlights section, a relatively short section that will describe the most critical information. Better education is a high priority. "We're looking into better ways to educate the public and doctors about changes in risk information, and to get information out faster," says Honig.

But FDA experts say the agency can't do it alone. The FDA judges drug risks for a population, doctors judge risks for individual patients, and patients judge the risks they'll take based on personal values. Ultimately, drug safety requires involvement of all parts of the health system.

11

Drug Manufacturers Should Disclose All Clinical Trial Results

Edward J. Markey

Congressman Edward J. Markey, a Democrat, represents the Seventh District of Massachusetts in the U.S. House of Representatives.

In order to make safe and effective decisions regarding health care, patients and physicians need access to complete and accurate medical information. However, investigations have revealed that some pharmaceutical companies withheld vital information about the potentially dangerous side effects of certain antidepressants. It is possible that some of the companies intentionally hid the results of their clinical trials because they were worried that publicity about harmful side effects would hurt their profits. In order to make sure that the doctors who prescribe medicine and their patients have access to all available information about clinical trials, the Fair Access to Clinical Trials (FACT) Act has been introduced in Congress. The FACT Act would require drug companies to register and make public all of their clinical trials and to report the results of those trials. The registry will help improve prescription drug safety and give consumers the information they need to protect their health and safety.

M r. Speaker, I rise today to introduce the Fair Access to Clinical Trials (FACT) Act.[1] This bill is designed to ensure

1. As of November 2005, the FACT Act was still under consideration in Congress.

Edward J. Markey, statement of introduction of the Fair Access to Clinical Trials (FACT) Act before the U.S. Congress, Washington, DC, October 7, 2004.

72

that the public has complete and accurate information about the drugs and devices they use.

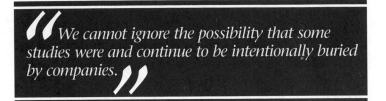

We cannot ignore the possibility that some studies were and continue to be intentionally buried by companies.

Recent revelations in the press and in the oversight hearings conducted by the Energy and Commerce Committee's Oversight and Investigations Subcommittee have raised serious concerns that some companies in the pharmaceutical and medical device industries have failed to properly disclose important information to the public about the safety of certain drugs or medical devices. For example, there is now evidence that several pediatric anti-depressant trials that produced important new adverse information about the safety of certain drugs were not released to the public. The public is now demanding to know why these trials never saw the light of day. Although much attention has focused on disclosure problems involving the effects of certain anti-depressants on young people, the problem of selective disclosure and publication is not limited to a specific type of drug or scenario—the same concerns exist whether we are talking about drugs to treat depression, heart disease or arthritis, or even a medical device that would be implanted into the human body.

Disclosure Is Necessary for Public Safety

I am sure that some clinical trials do not become part of the medical literature for innocent reasons. But we cannot ignore the possibility that some studies were and continue to be intentionally buried by companies who are worried about the impact of a negative trial on their bottom line. Regardless of the motivation, however, the fact remains that we don't know what trials are currently being conducted, so it is impossible to determine whether the companies and researchers are actually telling us the whole truth about their drugs and devices or whether they are painting a distorted picture of their products by picking and choosing which trials they want to reveal.

This creates two huge problems.

The first is that in order for doctors to make good medical decisions and provide their patients with the best possible care, they need to have access to complete and sound scientific data.

The second is that when people enroll in a clinical trial they give up a certain control of their own personal medical decisions, willingly taking experimental drugs and subjecting themselves to potential harm in the belief that their participation in the studies will add to the advancement of medical knowledge and potentially unlock the secrets of disease. But if a researcher or a company that sponsors a trial does not publicize the results, the knowledge gained from putting those participants at risk remains forever buried in some researcher's computer. That information will not be available to doctors, or to other medical researchers, who could use it.

Registration of Drug Trials
Should Be Mandatory

In order to ensure that clinicians have all the information they need in order to make sound medical decisions, uphold the ethical responsibility to patients and protect public health, I am proud to join with the gentleman from California, Mr. [Henry] Waxman [representative from the 30th District of California], to introduce the Fair Access to Clinical Trials (the FACT Act) a bill to create a mandatory, public, federal registry of all clinical trials.

> *In order for doctors to make good medical decisions and provide their patients with the best possible care, they need to have access to complete and sound scientific data.*

The FACT act will require researchers to register their clinical trials in a federal registry before starting them and report the results of those trials at the conclusion. The federal database will include both federal-funded and privately-funded clinical trials so that clinicians, patients and researchers will be able to know the universe of clinical trials on a particular drug and have access to the results of those trials. Our bill also establishes strong enforcement mechanisms, including monetary penalties of up to $10,000 per day for manufacturers who refuse to comply.

The registry established under the bill is intended to meet all of the minimum criteria for a trial registry set out by the International Committee of Medical Journal Editors, and will satisfy the American Medical Association's call for the results of all clinical trials to be publicly available to doctors and patients. Our legislation has been endorsed by the *New England Journal of Medicine* and the Elizabeth Glaser Pediatric AIDS Foundation.

The FACT Act will ensure that patients have the tools they need to make informed decisions, maintain the integrity of the medical community, and protect the health of their patients and our families.

I look forward to working with everyone concerned about this important issue so that we end up with a system that preserves a robust system of research and ensures a robust system of disclosure.

12

Drug Manufacturers Do Not Hide Clinical Trial Results

Caroline Loew

Caroline Loew is vice president of scientific and regulatory affairs at the Pharmaceutical Research and Manufacturers of America, also known as PhRMA.

The Pharmaceutical Research and Manufacturers of America (PhRMA), which comprises sixty-seven preeminent research-based pharmaceutical and biotechnology companies, invests billions of dollars to research and develop new medicines. Contrary to the current negative opinion of the pharmaceutical industry, PhRMA companies are committed to improving the lives of patients and disclosing all relevant information—positive or negative—from clinical studies of marketed drugs. This information is communicated through medical journals, public scientific meetings, and Web site postings. With the understanding that these methods of communication might reach a limited group of people, PhRMA also has established an Internet database to make clinical drug trial results more accessible to the general public. PhRMA and its member companies make every effort to ensure physicians and patients have access to comprehensive information regarding prescription drug studies.

PhRMA [Pharmaceutical Research and Manufacturers of America] member companies are firmly committed to communicating meaningful results of all controlled clinical trials of

Caroline Loew, testimony before the U.S. House Subcommittee on Oversight and Investigations, Committee on Energy and Commerce, Washington, DC, September 9, 2004.

marketed drugs—regardless of outcome. This means that results will be communicated if they are positive, negative, or anywhere in between. While these disclosures of negative results may not make splashy headlines or conform to the current negative view of the pharmaceutical industry, they are made every day by this industry. One recent example is the disclosure of the results of a multi-year head-to-head trial involving two well-known cholesterol-lowering agents, even though the results did not support the marketing position of the sponsor of the trial.

Commitment to Disclose

And this commitment to transparency is not new. Two years ago [2002], the PhRMA board of directors approved a set of voluntary *Principles on Conduct of Clinical Trials and Communication of Clinical Trial Results (the Principles)*. These *Principles*, which have been in effect since October 1, 2002, express in straightforward language the commitment of PhRMA-member companies to communicate the results of clinical trials, both positive and negative:

> We commit to timely communication of meaningful results of controlled clinical trials of marketed products or investigational products that are approved for marketing, regardless of outcome.

To strengthen this commitment even further, the PhRMA executive committee approved at its June 2004 meeting additional "Questions and Answers" to clarify some of the concepts in the *Principles*. In particular, the *Principles* now state that PhRMA member companies commit to publish the results of "all hypothesis-testing clinical trials [they] conduct, regardless of outcome, for marketed products or investigational products that are approved for marketing." Significantly, the *Principles* clearly state that results should be communicated regardless of whether they are positive or negative. . . .

Limited Methods of Communication

The *Principles* encourage sponsors to communicate clinical trial results by means of publication in a peer-reviewed medical journal, such as the *New England Journal of Medicine*, but recognize that manufacturers do not control which studies get published and that not all studies will merit publication in a peer-reviewed journal. The *Principles* thus provide for alternate methods of communication, such as through presentation at a public scientific meeting or posting the results on a website.

Results will be communicated if they are positive, negative, or anywhere in between.

One difficulty with these alternative methods of communication is they often only reach a limited audience, such as the physicians who attend a particular meeting. PhRMA believes an appropriately designed internet database could solve this problem. By providing a central, widely accessible repository for clinical study results and a standardized format for the reporting of such results, a clinical study results database could serve the valuable function of making clinical trial results more transparent and accessible. More importantly, in our opinion, this could be a valuable resource to support practicing physicians and their patients.

Clinical Study Results Database

Consequently, I am pleased to inform this subcommittee that the PhRMA board of directors recently approved the establishment of a Clinical Study Results Database. The database is a central, widely accessible, web-based repository for clinical study results in a user-friendly, standardized format. This database will serve the valuable function of making clinical study results for U.S. marketed pharmaceuticals more transparent.

The database will contain the results from all "hypothesis-testing" clinical studies completed since October 1, 2002—the implementation date of the PhRMA *Principles*—for drug products that are approved in the United States. This will include both positive and negative results by providing a bibliography of published articles and unpublished clinical study summaries. In short, the database will contain information that is consistent with the PhRMA Principles, i.e., the results of all hypothesis-testing clinical trials, regardless of outcome, for marketed drugs or investigational drugs that are approved for marketing.

The information on the database will be presented in a standard format that is easily searchable and includes the sponsoring company's name, the proprietary and generic names of the drug, a link or reference to the FDA-approved drug label, the studied indication(s), a bibliography of published studies together with a link (where available) to the printed articles, and a summary of the results of clinical studies that have not been published.

We commit to timely communication of meaningful results of controlled clinical trials . . . regardless of outcome.

This summary of unpublished results will be presented in a standard format accepted by regulators in the United States, Europe and Japan—the International Conference on Harmonization's (ICH) E-3 guidance on the structure and content of clinical study reports. This will provide scientific information about the results of a study in a standard, non-promotional manner that doctors can understand. It will include basic information about the study and its results, such as the design of the trial, the number of patients studied, the dose and mode of administration, and a summary of conclusions and outcomes on the safety and efficacy of the drug.

Limitations of the Database

As we implement the database, we are addressing several important regulatory and policy issues. For example, while PhRMA supports both the free flow of scientific information and the practice of medicine, PhRMA wants to ensure that the information in the database is not considered a substitute for the FDA-approved prescribing information. Thus, while it is important that the information in a results database be comprehensive and presented in a manner that is useful to physicians seeking additional information about a drug product, we think it is equally important that users understand the limitations of the database. The website thus will include a notice stressing that the database is being made available for informational purposes only and that the full prescribing information approved by the FDA should be the physician's primary source of information about the use of every medicine. In addition, the database will provide a link to the drug's full prescribing information.

We also want to ensure that the database is useful for practicing physicians. During the past few months, we have consulted with several physician groups, including the American Medical Association (AMA), the American Psychiatric Association, and others. While we do not want to speak for any of these groups, we are optimistic that we are heading in the right direction. We realize, however, that it will be critical to obtain ongoing feedback from these groups and from individual physicians and patients once the site is up and running. For that reason, the site will have a web-based form so users can comment on the utility of the database. We look forward to using this feedback to improve the site over the coming months.

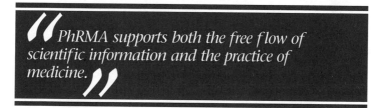

PhRMA supports both the free flow of scientific information and the practice of medicine.

Finally, PhRMA believes a database will be most useful if it is administered in partnership with or by an independent third party. We thus plan to explore the possibility of partnering with an independent group to actually administer the database. Because we are committed to establishing a database as quickly as possible, however, we do not intend to wait for a third party before initiating the program. On the contrary, we plan to establish the database, at least initially, as a PhRMA project to ensure it is up and running and available to practicing physicians in a timely manner. We will then seek to transition the program once an appropriate partner or independent third party has been identified.

PhRMA also believes that the need for rapid deployment of a database counsels against government involvement at this time. For instance, the registry authorized by Section 113 of FDAMA [FDA Modernization Act (1997)] was not fully implemented by the National Library of Medicine until nearly five years after passage of the authorizing legislation. We do not believe it is in anybody's interest to delay implementation of a results database in a similar fashion.

PhRMA is taking a leadership role on this issue and plans to have its Clinical Study Results Database operational and available for public use on October 1, 2004.[1] However, we realize that this is no small undertaking and expect that it may take up to a year before all relevant information is incorporated, especially clinical study information from complex multi-national phase IV studies.

In sum, PhRMA and its member companies are firmly committed to the value of transparency of clinical trial information. We are excited about our initiative to establish the Clinical Study Results Database and anticipate rapid progress in the coming weeks.

1. The database is now available at www.clinicalstudyresults.org.

13

Overaggressive Marketing of Vioxx Put Patients at Risk

Economist

The Economist *is a weekly international newsmagazine based in London.*

In August 2005 a jury in Texas awarded $253 million in damages to the widow of a man who died of a heart arrhythmia after using the pain reliever Vioxx for less than a year. More than four thousand additional cases against Vioxx manufacturer Merck have been filed. While Vioxx is a useful drug for many, one of its side effects is an increased risk of heart problems. This case has caused public distrust and increased scrutiny regarding how drug companies market their products. Merck aggressively marketed Vioxx to doctors and patients, with the result that patients who could have taken other pain relievers were prescribed Vioxx and exposed to its cardiovascular risks. In light of the Vioxx controversy, drug manufacturers need to become more forthcoming about their products' risks and benefits. In addition, to regain the trust of consumers, drug companies should focus their resources on the research of new treatments—rather than on marketing.

For medicines that were meant to relieve pain, Vioxx and its relatives—a new generation of anti-inflammatory drugs called the COX-2 inhibitors—are causing spasms all round.

Since Merck withdrew Vioxx from sale late last year [2004] because of its association with an increased risk of nasty cardiovascular side-effects, sharp questions have been asked about how big drug firms communicate risks to the wider world, how they market their wares and how effective government regulators are in policing the industry. The American public now seems to distrust the very firms that are supposed to be helping to lead the fight against disease.

The Verdict Against Merck Reflects the Public's Outrage

The latest example of this came last week [August 2005] in Texas, where a jury awarded the widow of a man who died of a heart arrhythmia, having taken Vioxx for less than a year, $253 million in damages. Merck rightly argues that the scientific facts of the case do not support this verdict, and has vowed to appeal the decision.

In any event, the award will be reduced vastly under Texas law. And yet the verdict, even if overturned, is symptomatic of public attitudes. The jurors were outraged at evidence that Merck may have known of the risks of Vioxx years before it revealed them. The Texas case is only one of more than 4,000 filed against Merck on Vioxx. Whatever happens in those cases, Merck, like all big drug firms, now faces closer scrutiny and, probably, tighter regulation in America.

This should force the big drug firms to change their business models, sooner rather than later. That is bound to be painful. These firms have been among the most profitable in the world, and much of their profit has been earned in America, where prices are highest. But if they are to continue to thrive, and generate new drugs in the future, they need to move quickly.

Direct Drug Advertising Can Mislead Consumers

Part of the drug firms' problem is that they have not, in fact, been generating enough new drugs. As the flow of genuinely original treatments has slowed to a trickle, the new drugs they have brought to market have tended to resemble those already on sale. The firms have pushed these with massive marketing efforts, aimed at both doctors and patients, reaching the latter with direct-to-consumer advertising on prime-time television and other media.

The irony of Vioxx is that such blockbuster marketing, intended to bring the drug to as many people as possible, has taken it out of the reach of all. Vioxx is not a bad medicine—in fact it is a useful drug for certain patients who suffer dangerous side-effects from other painkillers. But aggressive marketing meant that those who could have found relief on other drugs were given Vioxx and exposed to its risks.

The Vioxx episode has proven so painful for Merck that there are signs other drug makers are learning from it. The industry's American trade body, PhRMA, has announced guidelines with a view to more balanced communication of a drug's risks and benefits.

Some firms have gone further. Pfizer has said it will air ads for Viagra only during programs for which at least 90 percent of viewers are adults—so goodbye Superbowl. Bristol-Myers Squibb has promised to refrain from advertising its drugs during their first year on the market.

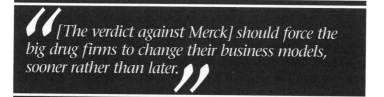

[The verdict against Merck] should force the big drug firms to change their business models, sooner rather than later.

There are signs, too, that the companies are starting to reconsider the way they sell drugs to doctors, after a backlash against the customary "food, flattery and friendship" on offer. Indeed, they may have little choice. More of the drugs to emerge from their labs in the future are likely to be for diseases such as cancer, which require detailed marketing to medical specialists for select populations.

Drug Companies Should Focus on Research—Not on Marketing

And in the longer term the drug industry will have to exploit the trend in medicine toward more personalized treatments. These are being driven by advances in genetics, which will make possible much more accurate diagnoses, and more tailored drugs, for much smaller groups of people. For these kinds of drugs, mass-consumer marketing will be even more inappropriate than it was for Vioxx. The days of the blockbuster drug are numbered.

In the wake of Vioxx and other controversial episodes, the big drug firms not only have to find a better way to market their wares, but also to rebuild their reputations with growing numbers of skeptical Americans. The best way to do that is to refocus their resources on research rather than marketing, and to come up with genuinely new treatments and more appropriate advice about how to use them. The future of pharmaceuticals lies in drugs that treat not just symptoms, but the underlying cause of a disorder. The pharmaceutical industry should settle for no less a remedy for its own condition.

14

Fraudulent Internet Pharmacies Sell Addictive Prescription Drugs

Gilbert M. Gaul and Mary Pat Flaherty

Gilbert M. Gaul and Mary Pat Flaherty work in the investigative unit of the Washington Post. *Both reporters have won Pulitzer prizes for their work.*

Internet pharmacies with little or no medical supervision are providing thousands of customers with a vast array of painkillers, antidepressants, and other addictive drugs that normally require a prescription. All that is needed is a simple telephone consultation between a patient and an unscrupulous doctor; the doctor writes a prescription and sends it electronically to the Internet pharmacy, which then ships the pills to the customer. No physical examination, lab tests, or medical follow-up is involved. Understaffed federal prosecutors are unable to stop the surge in this illegal drug trafficking over the Internet and are frustrated with the deaths, overdoses, and devastation that result.

In July 2001, regulators at the Nevada State Board of Pharmacy noticed something unusual among the reams of data that flow into the busy agency each day. Buried along with the other numbers was a report from a small Internet pharmacy that had filled 1,105 prescriptions for painkillers and other dangerous drugs that month.

The same tiny pharmacy had dispensed just 17 prescriptions in the prior six months.

Virtually overnight, prescriptiononline.com had become one of the largest distributors of controlled substances in Nevada. Over the next year, the online pharmacy shipped nearly 5 million doses of highly addictive drugs to customers scattered across the country. By the time regulators shut the Las Vegas firm in January [2002], prescriptiononline.com accounted for 10 percent of all hydrocodone sold in Nevada, regulators said.

It turned out that the booming business was owned by a 23-year-old former restaurant hostess. But it was run by her father, who had been convicted of a felony in 1992.

"For any single pharmacy to account for 10 percent of any drug is incredible," said Louis Ling, general counsel to the Nevada pharmacy board. "The fact that it was a highly addictive painkiller and an Internet site run by a convicted felon was even more troubling. This was unlike anything we had ever seen."

A Surge in Internet Drug Trafficking

With little notice or meaningful oversight, the Internet has become a pipeline for narcotics and other deadly drugs. Customers can pick from a vast array of painkillers, antidepressants, stimulants and steroids with few controls and virtually no medical monitoring.

There are dozens of legitimate online drugstores and mail-order pharmacies. Unlike rogue sites, they require customers to mail in prescriptions from their doctors. Typically, the legitimate sites offer a full range of medications, with painkillers accounting for less than 20 percent of their business.

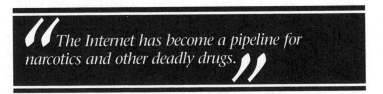

The Internet has become a pipeline for narcotics and other deadly drugs.

In contrast, a majority of the rogue sites' sales are for hydrocodone, Xanax, Valium and a few other addictive drugs. Many work with middlemen who set up the sites' customers with doctors who are veritable scrip-writing machines. Some of those doctors have financial problems and histories of substance abuse or medical incompetence, records show.

The online merchants now feed a sprawling shadow market for prescription drugs, frustrating medical leaders alarmed by the threat to public health and investigators hard-pressed to keep up with nimble Web sites that can open and close at a moment's notice.

"It's like rabbits," said Wayne A. Michaels, a senior investigator for the Drug Enforcement Administration [DEA]. "Every day, there are more of them. They're up, they're down, they're foreign, they're domestic."

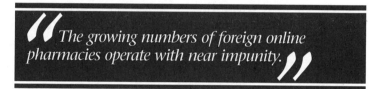

The growing numbers of foreign online pharmacies operate with near impunity.

The agency recently created a six-person task force solely to track the online trade in narcotics. But officials acknowledged the effort is a form of "triage" amid an escalating crisis. "We're afraid it's going to overwhelm us, once we've identified all these sites," said Elizabeth A. Willis, chief of the DEA's drug operations section.

The multimillion-dollar industry has appeared overnight, pumping millions of pills into some of America's smallest and most economically distressed communities.

The *Washington Post* obtained and analyzed a Nevada pharmacy board database of 30,000 orders filled by prescriptiononline.com. The analysis found that four of every 10 pills poured into four southern states with widely documented prescription-abuse problems. A disproportionate share of those drugs went to customers in small towns.

Some small Tennessee towns received 50 times more painkillers per capita than large cities, the analysis found. For example, Church Hill got 1,013 pills for every 1,000 residents; Nashville, just 26. Bristol got 1,584; Memphis, 14.

"It's a no-brainer why you see high volumes in these little places," said Tammy Meade, a narcotics prosecutor in Nashville. "Users and people who want to get their hands on enough to distribute can't doctor shop in places like that. And if they use the Internet, someone like me . . . is going to have a tougher time finding out."

No Medical Supervision

Stretching from Florida to California, the Internet pipeline has left a trail of deaths, overdoses, addictions and emotionally devastated families.

"It absolutely blew my mind that you could get these drugs online," said Sue R. Townsend, the coroner in Aiken County, S.C. Her son Douglas, 30, died after driving his car into a fence in September 2001. His family said he had taken a generic form of the tranquilizer Xanax, which they said he had purchased from myprivatedoc.com, a now-defunct Web site in Mesa, Ariz. Townsend's family sued the Web site, the pharmacy and the Arizona doctor who wrote the prescription, accusing them of selling the drug without a proper medical consultation. The case was recently settled with no admission of liability.

"Losing Doug has broken our hearts," Sue Townsend said, fighting back tears. "He had a young wife and a baby boy who will never know his daddy. Somehow we have to tell how dangerous this is, because it's happening all over."

In a typical purchase from a rogue site, a customer logs on and orders hydrocodone (generic Vicodin and Lortab). The Web site steers him to a middleman, often another Web site, which arranges a telephone consultation with a doctor. The customer and the doctor talk briefly, after which the doctor writes the prescription and sends it electronically to the Internet pharmacy. The pharmacy ships 60 pills to the customer by overnight mail. Total cost: $290. The pharmacy pockets $190 for the hydrocodone and the doctor and the middleman split the remaining $100 as a consultation fee. There are no face-to-face meetings, lab tests, X-rays or follow-ups.

Federal Prosecutors Cannot Keep Up

There are dozens of Web sites selling narcotics in the United States, with scores more operating offshore. Federal prosecutors have shut Web sites, filed indictments and won guilty pleas from several owners. But it often takes years to prove a case. In the meantime, the pills move.

For each site closed, "two or three more open," said Jennifer Bolen, a former federal prosecutor in Knoxville, Tenn. "It is so easy for them to close down a site one day and open a new one the next."

For the DEA, an agency already responsible for everything from drug cartels to street drugs, trying to police the growing number of online pharmacies "is like trying to work every corner drug dealer," said Laura M. Nagel, the agency's deputy assistant administrator. "We can't do it all."

When prosecutors shut the Internet pharmacy operations at thepillbox.com in San Antonio, much of the business shifted to prescriptiononline.com in Las Vegas, records show. When that site was closed two years later, Nevada regulators suspect the business shifted yet again—this time to Florida.

Some Web sites have dozens or even hundreds of affiliate sites. Others are designed to appear as though they are headquartered in the United States when they are really offshore, in such places as Namibia, Thailand and Sri Lanka. The growing numbers of foreign online pharmacies operate with near impunity. The Food and Drug Administration's [FDA] strongest recourse is to send a warning letter, which usually is ignored.

"As an investigator, it's incredibly frustrating," said Robert J. West, a special agent with the FDA's Office of Criminal Investigations. "All we can do is bang away and try to draw attention to what these guys are doing. Right now, I don't think people have any idea how widespread or dangerous this is."

Little Regulation

States regulate pharmacies, creating widely different rules governing Internet sites. Under-staffed pharmacy boards barely have time to inspect brick-and-mortar pharmacies, let alone virtual ones. Many online pharmacies have ignored state efforts to register them. Only one state—California—has a full-time agent investigating doctors writing prescriptions for Internet pharmacies.

The lax oversight comes amid Congress's inability to pass legislation requiring even minimal disclosure by Internet pharmacies.

In 1999, then-Rep. Ron Klink (D-Pa.) issued a warning at a committee hearing: "I am concerned a 'Wild West' world is unfolding before us, where many consumers are accessing potentially dangerous drugs with little or no practical guidance. Yet because it is e-commerce, there is a mentality: It must be progress."

In 2000, the FDA, the General Accounting Office and several House members urged that online pharmacies be required to disclose their owners, locations, doctors, affiliated pharmacies and telephone numbers. But Congress never followed through. Nearly four years later, there is still no disclosure requirement.

"Getting a bill regulating the Internet is about as hard as it gets," said William K. Hubbard, the FDA's senior associate commissioner. "You have all of these people worrying about stifling this wonderful thing . . . and they don't want the bad Feds in there."

A *Post* reporter sent e-mail asking for identifying information to 15 online pharmacies specializing in painkillers. Only one responded. It declined to say who owns the site or where it is located. One online pharmacy included a telephone number for customer service that linked to a freight forwarding company in Miami. When a reporter called, a secretary said that it moved shipments for a customer in Costa Rica.

In late 1999, the National Association of Boards of Pharmacy instituted a voluntary system for certifying online pharmacies, including inspections and disclosure. But of the hundreds of Internet pharmacies now operating, only a "dozen or so" signed up, said Carmen Catizone, the board's executive director. Most of those are large, legitimate sites, such as drugstore.com.

One pharmacy that received certification was prescription online.com. "I can't explain what happened there," Catizone said. "I know we certified it originally, and then later on we got some complaints, and we suspended their certification. Obviously, if we knew then what we do now, we never would have certified them.". . .

Easy to Abuse

One of prescriptiononline.com's customers was Nancy Harler, a former nurse, of Columbia, S.C. She had been getting her painkillers from thepillbox.com. But after that site's legal problems arose, prescriptiononline.com began filling her orders for hydrocodone.

> *Getting a bill regulating the Internet is about as hard as it gets.*

Harler said she had started ordering hydrocodone online for migraines and arthritis in February 2000. In all, she estimated that she spent $10,000 and used more than 1,500 pills. "It just got to the point where I was no longer in control and knew I needed help," she said.

Harler is now undergoing methadone treatment for her addiction, which she said was fed by the online pharmacies. "If you ask them anything about the money, they say we'll be glad to pull the plug. They know they have addicts on the line," she said.

Most of prescriptiononline.com's customers sought painkillers. The *Post's* analysis showed nearly 90 percent of the orders were for controlled substances, including hydrocodone and the generic equivalents of Valium and Xanax.

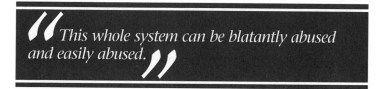

This whole system can be blatantly abused and easily abused.

For years, hydrocodone has been one of the most used and abused drugs, according to the DEA. Sales have soared, and so have thefts of the drug and hydrocodone-related emergency room admissions.

The street value of hydrocodone is also climbing, said Tony King, the agent in charge of the DEA's Louisville office. A single generic tablet that costs an online pharmacy 15 cents may be sold to Internet customers for $1.50. On the street, that same tablet may go for "$3 to $5," King said. Overall sales of hydrocodone in Kentucky have doubled in the past four years, to 120 million tablets.

The surge began a few years back, when doctors alarmed by OxyContin abuse began switching patients to hydrocodone, King said. "But hydrocodone is equally dangerous," he said. "It's kind of like: Do you use a .38- or .40-caliber gun to shoot yourself?"

A breakdown of prescriptiononline.com's sales by Zip code revealed that four of every 10 pills flowed into Alabama, Tennessee, Louisiana and Kentucky. Those four states routinely rank among the top five nationally in the per-capita use of hydrocodone and Xanax, according to law enforcement data.

The pills poured into small towns. In Hope, Ky., with a population of 152, customers bought 7,910 pills—an average of 52 pills for each resident. In Gunlock, Ky., population 430, customers bought 2,910 pills, about seven per person. By contrast, in Louisville, Kentucky's biggest city with a population of 206,239, customers bought 5,810 pills, about 0.03 per person.

In some cases, these orders went to multiple customers listed at the same address. For example, over five months 2,030 pills were shipped to five customers at one home in Baileyton, Ala. More than 80 percent were hydrocodone.

In an interview, [Jon S.] Opsahl, the California physician who wrote the prescriptions, said he was aware that customers occasionally listed the same address, but not to the extent detailed in the *Post* analysis. "I didn't have that data at the time," he said, calling the information "very disturbing. You've presented some information that certainly gives me some pause how this whole system can be blatantly abused and easily abused."

Still, Opsahl maintained that most Internet patients have legitimate needs.

That view is not shared by Mike Vories, a physician who runs a pain management clinic in Hazzard, Ky.

"How in the world does an Internet Web site have any control over whether that controlled substance is going to a patient with a legitimate complaint?" he wondered. "Really, come on. Let's call this for what it is. A few maybe are legitimate and have pain. For the majority, it is a source of income."

15

Young People Abuse Prescription Drugs

Donna Leinwand

Donna Leinwand, a reporter for USA Today, *serves on the National Press Club Board of Governors. She has also reported for the* Miami Herald *and Gannett News Service Washington Bureau.*

Prescription drug abuse among teenagers and young adults is rising at such an alarming rate that researchers are examining the cause. Contrary to popular belief, the reason is not always just to get high. Studies have shown that many college students with high academic standards medicate themselves to alleviate the stress. Researchers have also found that many students who take prescription drugs illicitly do so to relieve pain rather than to feel euphoric. Regardless of their motivation for abusing prescription drugs, young people are at a great risk of becoming addicted to these drugs and overdosing.

Daniel Ashkenazy, a promising pre-law student at the University of California, San Diego, had planned to fly home to the San Francisco Bay Area to see his visiting grandparents on Jan. 14 [2005]. Instead, he died that day after taking the addictive painkiller OxyContin and then drinking alcohol at a fraternity rush party.

Daniel's mother, Pamela Ashkenazy, found her son's misuse of a prescription drug puzzling. Daniel, 20, had a 3.8 grade-point average his junior year. He spoke with her nearly every day. He didn't seem to fit the profile of a young person who might drift into drug abuse, she said. But in the four months since Daniel's death, Ashkenazy has reached a different conclusion about the type of teens and young adults who abuse prescription drugs.

"I believe that those kids who are high achievers are the kids who are at risk," she says. "Parents think if they are raising their kids in affluent homes, if their kids are getting good grades, nothing is wrong. Well, none of that protected him."

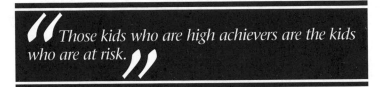

Those kids who are high achievers are the kids who are at risk.

The Ashkenazy case reflects what various university researchers are finding as they begin to examine an emerging boom in prescription-drug abuse among young adults and teenagers: Many of those who misuse narcotic pain relievers such as OxyContin or Vicodin, or stimulants such as Ritalin, are doing so not necessarily to get high, but also to ease stress or to try to improve academic performance.

Popular Pills

Prescription drugs most often abused by teenagers and young adults include:

• Ritalin. A mild stimulant often prescribed to children to treat attention deficit disorder (ADD), attention deficit hyperactivity disorder (ADHD) and narcolepsy. Abusers take it to suppress appetite, stay awake and feel euphoric.

• OxyContin. A strong pain reliever similar to morphine. Highly addictive, it is designed to be absorbed gradually. Crushing or chewing pills can cause a large amount of oxycodone, the active ingredient, to be released at once. That creates the potential for a dangerous or fatal overdose.

• Vicodin. A strong pain reliever that can be addictive. It is particularly popular among young adults. Its use among professional athletes was spotlighted when Green Bay Packers quarterback Brett Favre was treated for an addiction to the drug in 1996.

• Percocet. A painkiller that can be addictive. It's often given to patients who have undergone surgery.

• Morphine. Another addictive painkiller that is known for its use on patients who have undergone surgery. It is a base ingredient for many other painkillers, including OxyContin.

Patterns of Use and Abuse

Recent nationwide surveys by the University of Michigan and other researchers have indicated that the abuse of prescription drugs among young adults and teens is increasing, while the abuse of drugs such as cocaine and heroin is decreasing among those groups. The studies have said that about 6.7 million people ages 12–25 took a prescription drug for non-medical purposes during the previous year. Among illicit drugs, only marijuana had more users in that age group, about 12.8 million.

On Wednesday [May 18, 2005], the Society for Prevention Research, a group of scientists who examine drug abuse and recommend ways to counter it, presented analyses and original research based on such data collected during the past three years. Carol Boyd, director of the Institute for Research on Women and Gender at the University of Michigan, said researchers are beginning to understand which youths abuse prescription drugs, why they do so and where they get the drugs.

Sean Esteban McCabe, interim director of the Substance Abuse Research Center at the University of Michigan, said his colleagues' examination of drug use among college students found that "competitive" universities—those with high academic standards—reported higher rates of illicit use of prescription drugs.

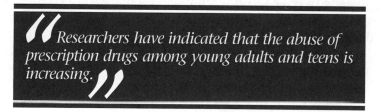

Researchers have indicated that the abuse of prescription drugs among young adults and teens is increasing.

McCabe did not identify specific campuses with high usage rates. However, he said researchers have found students are more likely to abuse prescription drugs if they are white, live in a fraternity or sorority house and have lower than a "B" average.

McCabe also found that young women who used prescription drugs illicitly usually got them from family members, particularly parents, while young men who used such drugs without prescriptions usually got them from friends.

Meanwhile, Boyd surveyed 1,017 middle and high school students in a Detroit-area public school district. Almost half the children had legitimate prescriptions for Ritalin and other medications. Ritalin is a stimulant used to treat attention deficit disorder.

Reasons for Abuse

Among the students surveyed by Boyd's group, one in four with legitimate prescriptions said other kids had asked them for pills. One in five said they had sold or traded away at least one pill. Most of the students who reported using such drugs without a prescription—79%—said they had done so to relieve pain rather than to get high, Boyd says. About 11% said they took the drugs to get high.

Boyd says the survey indicates that "when we talk about this big boom in prescription-drug abuse, we have to talk about two different groups who are using the drugs for two different reasons."

In a separate study at the University of New Mexico, Gilbert Quintero and other researchers at the university's Center for Health Promotion and Disease Prevention recently interviewed 52 college students who said they had misused prescription drugs during the previous year.

Quintero found that many of the students medicated themselves to relieve stress. The students identified 58 different brand names of drugs they had misused. Vicodin was the most popular, with 65.4% saying they had used it without a prescription, followed by Percocet, the tranquilizers Valium and Xanax, and OxyContin.

Quintero quoted a 20-year-old woman who had misused Percocet, a painkiller. "It just relaxes me," she told the researchers. "It's a complete relaxer but you can still function and do other things. It's not like when you're drunk and totally out of it."

Some students said they took prescription drugs socially because they are cheaper than alcohol. One out of four students interviewed said they had misused Ritalin, primarily to keep up with academic demands, Quintero said.

Organizations to Contact

American Council on Science and Health (ACSH)
1995 Broadway, 2nd Fl., New York, NY 10023-5860
(212) 362-7044 • fax: (212) 362-4919
e-mail: acsh@acsh.org • Web site: www.acsh.org

ACSH is a consumer education group concerned with issues related to food, nutrition, chemicals, pharmaceuticals, lifestyle, the environment, and health. It publishes the quarterly newsletter *Priorities* as well as reports such as "Patient Safety Research: Creating Crisis."

American Holistic Medical Association (AHMA)
12101 Menaul Blvd. NE, Suite C, Albuquerque, NM 87112
(505) 292-7788 • fax: (505) 293-7582
Web site: www.holisticmedicine.org

AHMA promotes the practice of holistic health care, a concept that emphasizes the integration of physical, mental, emotional, and spiritual concerns with environmental harmony. It publishes a quarterly newsletter.

American Medical Association (AMA)
515 N. State St., Chicago, IL 60610
(800) 621-8335 • Web site: www.ama-assn.org

The AMA is the largest professional association for medical doctors. It helps set standards for medical education and practices, and it is a powerful lobby in Washington for physicians' interests. The association publishes journals for many medical fields, including the monthly *Archives of Surgery* and the weekly *JAMA*.

American Public Health Association (APHA)
800 I St. NW, Washington, DC 20001
(202) 777-2742 • fax: (202) 777-2534
e-mail: comments@apha.org • Web site: www.apha.org

Founded in 1872, the American Public Health Association consists of over fifty thousand individuals and organizations that aim to improve public health. Its members represent over fifty public health occupations, including researchers, practitioners, administrators, teachers, and other health care workers. Some of APHA's publications include the monthly *American Journal of Public Health* and the books *Building Better Health, a Handbook of Behavioral Change* and *Health and Health Care 2010: The Forecast, the Challenge*.

Center for Drug Evaluation and Research (CDER)
5600 Fishers Lane, Rockville, MD 20857
(888) 463-6332
Web site: www.fda.gov/cder

The Center for Drug Evaluation and Research promotes and protects the health of Americans by assuring that all prescription and over-the-counter drugs are safe and effective. The center routinely monitors television, radio, and print drug advertisements to ensure that they are truthful and balanced. It publishes the *News Along the Pike* newsletter and the report "CDER 2003 Report to the Nation: Improving Public Health Through Human Drugs."

Healthcare Leadership Council (HLC)
1001 Pennsylvania Ave. NW, Suite 550 South, Washington, DC 20004
(202) 452-8700 • fax: (202) 296-9561
Web site: www.hlc.org

The council is a forum in which health care industry leaders can jointly develop policies, plans, and programs that support a market-based health care system. HLC believes America's health care system should value innovation and provide affordable high-quality health care free from excessive government regulations. It offers the latest press releases on health issues and various newsletters.

Health Care Problems Archive
PO Box 61115, Palo Alto, CA 94306
(650) 324-2425 • fax: (650) 329-1099
e-mail: lizparrott@healthcareproblems.org
Web site: http://healthcareproblems.org

The Health Care Problems Archive is a collection of accounts of problems with the U.S. health care system from people involved in every aspect of the system. The accounts are made available to all who are developing solutions to health care system problems, or who want to educate themselves about the problems. The archive contains many articles on prescription drugs.

Institute of Medicine
500 Fifth St. NW, Washington, DC 20001
(202) 334-2352 • fax: (202) 334-1412
e-mail: iomwww@nas.edu • Web site: www.iom.edu

The Institute of Medicine serves as adviser to the nation to improve health. As an independent, scientific adviser, the Institute of Medicine strives to provide advice that is unbiased, based on evidence, and grounded in science. It has published many reports on health care, including prescription drugs. These reports are available on its Web site.

National Association of Boards of Pharmacy (NABP)
1600 Feehanville Dr., Mount Prospect, IL 60056
(847) 391-4406 • fax: (847) 391-4502
Web site: www.nabp.net

The NABP is the only professional association that represents the state boards of pharmacy in all fifty United States, the District of Columbia, Guam, Puerto Rico, the Virgin Islands, New Zealand, eight Canadian provinces, two Australian states, and South Africa. It publishes the NABP newsletter to educate, inform, and communicate the objectives and programs of the association.

National Center for Complementary and Alternative Medicine (NCCAM)
PO Box 7923, Gaithersburg, MD 20898
(888) 644-6226 • fax: (866) 464-3616
e-mail: info@nccam.nih.gov • Web site: http://nccam.nih.gov

Congress established the NCCAM in 1998 to encourage and support research on complementary and alternative medicine (CAM). The center also provides information on CAM to health care providers and the public, evaluates the safety and effectiveness of popular herbal remedies and practices such as acupuncture, and supports studies to determine how CAM products interact with standard medications. NCCAM publishes consensus reports and fact sheets on various alternative treatments, cancer, and dietary supplements.

National Clearinghouse for Alcohol and Drug Information (NCADI)
PO Box 2345, Rockville, MD 20847-2345
(800) 729-6686 • fax: (301) 468-6433
e-mail: info@health.org • Web site: www.health.org

The National Clearinghouse for Alcohol and Drug Information, a service of the Substance Abuse and Mental Health Services Administration (SAMHSA), is the nation's resource for the most current and comprehensive information about substance abuse prevention and treatment. It distributes recent studies and surveys for the general public. NCADI produces the twice-monthly publication *Prevention Alert* with such titles as "Prevention Alert: Trouble in the Medicine Chest: Rx Drug Abuse Growing" and "Prevention Alert: Prescription Drug Abuse: What Can Be Done?"

National Coalition on Health Care
1200 G St. NW, Suite 750, Washington, DC 20005
(202) 638-7151
e-mail: dmurphy@nchc.org • Web site: www.nchc.org

The National Coalition on Health Care is a nonprofit, nonpartisan group that represents the nation's largest alliance working to improve America's health care and make it more affordable. The coalition offers several policy studies with titles ranging from "Building a Better Health System: Specifications for Reform" to "Reducing Medical Errors and Improving Patient Safety."

National Institute on Drug Abuse (NIDA)
6001 Executive Blvd., Room 5213, Bethesda, MD 20892-9561
(301) 443-1124
e-mail: information@lists.nida.nih.gov • Web site: http://nida.nih.gov

The mission of the National Institute on Drug Abuse is to lead the nation in bringing the power of science to bear on drug abuse and addiction. NIDA supports over 85 percent of the world's research on the health aspects of drug abuse and addiction. The institute's priorities are prevention research, treatment, and training. Its publications include the booklets *Principles of Drug Addiction Treatment: A Research-Based Guide* and *Preventing Drug Use Among Children and Adolescents: A Research-Based Guide for Parents, Educators, and Community Leaders.*

National Institutes of Health (NIH)
9000 Rockville Pike, Bethesda, MD 20892
(301) 496-4000
e-mail: nihinfo@od.nih.gov • Web site: www.nih.gov

A part of the U.S. Department of Health and Human Services, the NIH comprises twenty-seven separate components, including the National Human Genome Research Institute, and the National Cancer Institute. Its mission is to discover new knowledge that will improve everyone's health. In order to achieve this mission, the NIH conducts and supports research, helps train research investigators, and fosters the communication of medical information. The NIH also publishes online fact sheets, brochures, and handbooks.

National Pharmaceutical Council (NPC)
1894 Preston White Dr., Reston, VA 20191
(703) 620-6390
Web site: http://npcnow.org

Supported by more than twenty of the nation's major research-based pharmaceutical companies, NPC sponsors a variety of research and education projects aimed at demonstrating that the appropriate use of pharmaceuticals improves both patient treatment outcomes and the cost-effective delivery of overall health care services. Its publications include the reports "Are the Benefits of Newer Drugs Worth Their Cost?" and "Availability of New Drugs and Americans' Ability to Work."

Partnership for a Drug-Free America
405 Lexington Ave., Suite 1601, New York, NY 10174
(212) 922-1560 • fax: (212) 922-1570
Web site: www.drugfree.org

The Partnership for a Drug-Free America is a nonprofit coalition of communication, health, medical, and educational professionals working to reduce illicit drug use and help people live healthy, drug-free lives. It publishes news releases such as "Generation Rx: National Study Reveals New Category of Substance Abuse Emerging: Teens Abusing Rx and OTC Medications Intentionally to Get High" and "Prescription Medicine Misuse and Abuse: A Growing Problem."

Pharmaceutical Research and Manufacturers of America (PhRMA)
1100 Fifteenth St. NW, Washington, DC 20005
(202) 835-3400 • fax: (202) 835-3414
Web site: www.phrma.org

The Pharmaceutical Research and Manufacturers of America represents the country's leading pharmaceutical research and biotechnology companies. The mission of PhRMA is to conduct effective advocacy for public policies that encourage discovery of important new medicines. Its publications include *Pharmaceutical Industry Profile 2005—from Laboratory to Patient: Pathways to Biopharmaceutical Innovation* and *Why Do Medicines Cost So Much?*

Bibliography

Books

John Abramson

Overdosed America: The Broken Promise of American Medicine. New York: HarperCollins, 2004.

Marcia Angell

The Truth About the Drug Companies: How They Deceive Us and What to Do About It. New York: Random House, 2004.

Jerry Avorn

Powerful Medicines: The Benefits, Risks, and Costs of Prescription Drugs. New York: Knopf, 2004.

Donald L. Barlett and James B. Steele

Critical Condition: How Health Care in America Became Big Business—and Bad Medicine. New York: Doubleday, 2004.

Mark H. Beers

The Merck Manual of Medical Information, Second Edition: The World's Most Widely Used Medical Reference. New York: Pocket, 2003.

Jay S. Cohen

Over Dose: The Case Against the Drug Companies: Prescription Drugs, Side Effects, and Your Health. New York: Penguin Putnam, 2001.

Company Inc Medical et al.

The PDR Family Guide to Prescription Drugs, 9th Edition: America's Leading Drug Guide for over 50 Years. New York: Three Rivers Press, 2002.

Carl Elliott

Better than Well: American Medicine Meets the American Dream. New York: W.W. Norton, 2003.

Joan E. Gadsby

Addiction by Prescription. Toronto, Ontario: Key Porter Books, 2000.

Merrill Goozner

The $800 Million Pill: The Truth Behind the Cost of New Drugs. Berkeley and Los Angeles: University of California Press, 2004.

Katherine Greider

The Big Fix: How the Pharmaceutical Industry Rips Off American Consumers. New York: Public Affairs, 2003.

H. Winter Griffith

Complete Guide to Prescription and Nonprescription Drugs 2004. New York: Perigee Trade, 2003.

Icon Health Publications

The Official Patient's Sourcebook on Prescription Drug Dependence: A Revised and Updated Directory for the Internet Age. San Diego: Icon Health, 2005.

Jerome P. Kassirer

On the Take: How Medicine's Complicity with Big Business Can Endanger Your Health. New York: Oxford University Press, 2005.

Barry Meier — *Pain Killer: A "Wonder" Drug's Trail of Addiction and Death.* New York: Rodale Books, 2003.

Cindy R. Mogil — *Swallowing a Bitter Pill: How Prescription and Over-the-Counter Drug Abuse Is Ruining Lives—My Story.* Far Hills, NJ: New Horizon Press, 2001.

Rick Ng — *Drugs—from Discovery to Approval.* Hoboken, NJ: John Wiley & Sons, 2004.

Ross Pelton and James B. Lavalle — *Nutritional Cost of Prescription Drugs: How to Maintain Good Nutrition While Using Prescription Drugs.* Englewood, CO: Morton, 2000.

Drew Pinsky — *When Painkillers Become Dangerous: What Everyone Needs to Know About OxyContin and Other Prescription Drugs.* Center City, MN: Hazelden, 2004.

Douglas J. Pisano and David Mantus — *FDA Regulatory Affairs: A Guide for Prescription Drugs, Medical Devices, and Biologics.* Boca Raton, FL: CRC Press, 2003.

James J. Rybacki — *The Essential Guide to Prescription Drugs 2005.* New York: HarperResource, 2004.

Harold M. Silverman — *The Pill Book, Eleventh Edition.* New York: Bantam, 2004.

Carol Simontacchi — *Natural Alternatives to Vioxx, Celebrex & Other Anti-Inflammatory Prescription Drugs.* Garden City Park, NY: Square One, 2005.

Ray D. Strand — *Death by Prescription: The Shocking Truth Behind an Overmedicated Nation.* Nashville: Nelson Books, 2003.

Sid M. Wolfe — *Worst Pills, Best Pills: A Consumer's Guide to Avoiding Drug-Induced Death or Illness.* New York: Pocket, 2005.

Periodicals

Leila Abbond — "Drug-Pricing Rules Face Review," *Wall Street Journal,* May 24, 2004.

Giancarlo Barolat — "A New Battlefront in the War on Drugs," *USA Today Magazine,* March 2005.

Jarrett T. Barrios and Michael Festa — "A Free Market for Medicines," *Boston Globe,* September 21, 2003.

David Blumenthal — "Doctors and Drug Companies," *New England Journal of Medicine,* October 28, 2004.

Stuart Elliott and Nat Ives — "Selling Prescription Drugs to Consumers," *New York Times,* October 12, 2004.

Mary Pat Flaherty and Gilbert M. Gaul — "Millions of Americans Look Outside U.S. for Drugs: Desire for Low Prices Often Outweighs Obeying Law," *Washington Post,* October 23, 2003.

Faye Flam — "A Prescription for Full Disclosure: The Results of Clinical Trials of Many Drugs Are Going Unreported or Unnoticed, Which Flies in the Face of Science and May Even Harm Patients," *Philadelphia Inquirer*, August 15, 2004.

Judith Graham and Michael Higgins — "Prescription Drug Abuse on the Rise in America," *Chicago Tribune*, October 20, 2003.

Gardiner Harris — "Drug Companies Seek to Mend Their Image," *New York Times*, July 8, 2004.

Gardiner Harris — "Price of AIDS Drug Intensifies Debate on Legal Imports," *New York Times*, April 14, 2004.

Marc Kaufman — "FDA Officer Suggests Strict Curbs on 5 Drugs: Makers Dispute Claims About Health Risks," *Washington Post*, November 19, 2004.

Gina Kolata — "There's a Blurry Line Between Rx and O.T.C.," *New York Times*, December 21, 2003.

Francesca Lunzer Kritz — "FDA on Drug Ads: Less Is More," *Washington Post*, February 10, 2004.

Gregory M. Lamb — "A New Corporate Villain—Drugmakers?" *Christian Science Monitor*, September 20, 2004.

Los Angeles Times — "An Ailing, Failing FDA," November 23, 2004.

Los Angeles Times — "Open Door to Drug Imports," November 6, 2003.

Linda Loyd — "A Medicine Maze," *Philadelphia Inquirer*, May 2, 2004.

Amy Dockser Marcus — "Price Becomes Factor in Cancer Treatment: Costly 'Target' Drugs Extend Lives, but Confront Patients with Wrenching Choices," *Wall Street Journal*, September 7, 2004.

Vivian Marino — "To Make a Pill More Affordable, Cut It in Half," *New York Times*, April 13, 2004.

Barry Meier — "Results of Drug Trials Can Justify Doctors Through Omission," *New York Times*, July 21, 2004.

Barry Meier — "Two Studies, Two Results, and a Debate over a Drug," *New York Times*, June 3, 2004.

Alan Murray — "Drug Makers' Paths of Influence Need to Be Less Hidden," *Wall Street Journal*, November 11, 2003.

New York Times — "A Plan to Import Drugs Safely," November 1, 2003.

New York Times — "For Truth in Drug Trial Reporting," June 20, 2004.

Andrea Nurko — "Abuse of Prescription Medicine Afflicts 15 Million, Study Shows," *San Diego Union-Tribune*, July 8, 2005.

Tony Pugh "FDA Accused of Favoring Drug Industry," *Miami Herald*, October 15, 2003.

Christopher Rowland "Officials Take Steps to Curb Fake Drugs: Market for Counterfeit Seen Growing Quickly," *Boston Globe*, October 13, 2003.

Paul M. Rudolph and Ilisa B.G. Bernstein "Counterfeit Drugs," *New England Journal of Medicine*, April 1, 2004.

F.M. Scherer "The Pharmaceutical Industry—Prices and Progress," *New England Journal of Medicine*, August 26, 2004.

Robert Steinbrook "Public Registration of Clinical Trials," *New England Journal of Medicine*, July 22, 2004.

Bernadette Tansey "Citizens Use Law to Pursue Drug Firms: Citing Unfair Competition and Weak FDA Oversight, Consumer Coalition Sues Giant Pharmaceutical Companies," *San Francisco Chronicle*, November 23, 2003.

Heather Won Tesoriero "New Drug Problem: Getting Antidepressants: In Wake of FDA Warning, Some Parents Have Trouble Getting Prescriptions for Kids," *Wall Street Journal*, October 7, 2004.

Shankar Vedantam "FDA Told Its Analyst to Censor Data on Antidepressants," *Washington Post*, September 24, 2004.

Washington Post "Illegal Drugs," October 27, 2003.

Rob Waters "Drug Report Barred by FDA: Scientist Links Antidepressants to Suicide in Kids," *San Francisco Chronicle*, February 1, 2004.

Burton A. Weisbrod "Solving the Drug Dilemma," *Washington Post*, August 22, 2003.

Index